To Stephanie

It was good meeting you and talking with you. I wish you a joyous Christmas season and a wonderful New Year in 2004!

Roy McDonald
London
Dec. 22, 2003

Living: A London Journal

Ergo Productions

Living:
A London Journal
Roy McDonald

Copyright © Roy McDonald, 1978.
Fifth printing, September 1998.

Published by Ergo Productions, P.O. Box 1439, Station B, London, Ontario N6A 5M2.

Photography by R. Bondy.

All rights reserved, which includes the right to reproduce this book or portions thereof.

Printed and bound by the Porcupine's Quill Inc.

ISBN 0-920516-01-7

For Rose and

With heartfelt appreciation to my mother, Paul, Ken, Mary, and other good friends who have given me help, encouragement and inspiration in this project and in so many other ways.

Introduction

Running and jogging, for fitness in our long-suffering age of the automobile, are widely proselytized today. Now I walk a lot myself, appropriately enough, since my nickname as a kid was "turtle", not "antelope". But I do run in short bursts, occasionally, trying to keep up with Roy McDonald on his way to the bus stop, McDonald's, or other ports of call. Roy even handicaps himself because his perpetual companion is a satchel of books, for reference and sometimes for sale. And the McDonald satchel is heavy.

The thirty-or-so excess pounds that I carry are more evenly distributed over my body and I should run more smoothly than Roy, but such is not the case. More often than not, I have to watch him pull away out front. Needless to say, I am impressed with his power.

Roy's journal is also powerful as it weaves references to past alcoholic meanderings into the complex tapestry of a life reported on, while being lived. Of a life struggling, talking, loving, talking, losing, lusting, talking. Singed by the flame but reaffiriming a robust, tender gallantry. Indeed, Roy's 1976 seven day journal is a unique contribution to the journal tradition and illustrates the potential in journal-writing for each of us to record, reveal and reflect upon this experience of living.

Roy McDonald is peripatetic: physically, intellectually, and spiritually. His physical stage has its changing-house in London, Ontario, his home town. One side of the triangle leads to Toronto, the other to Montreal. But both also lead to each other and back to London. Roy has friends, friendly-acquaintances, and some nay-sayers in all three cities.

To be sure, some of the nay-sayers may be slightly-jealous husbands, boyfriends, or startled macho-types who have found that their women enjoy a McDonald kiss on the hand or an enthusiastic embrace when meeting Roy on the street, at an opening, or in a restaurant. Indeed, Roy has faced the negative and the positive cycles of human experience and survived them both. Profited from them both. And whatever one might say about Roy's public laying-on-of-hands on female flesh, it is not sneaky, though it may be underhanded. You see there is more to Roy McDonald than that.

Over the years, girls and women of varying ages have found a rare, sympathetic and empathetic friend in Roy. Letters he has received certainly prove that. And as for his male friends, those of us who have walked with him, caroused with him, had our sinuses cleared when he roared his ribald rage in the taverns and the streets, and talked with him about almost every topic under the sun and moon, we have found an incomparable friend for all seasons and the long haul.

Roy's journal refers to his daily meditations and the techniques of positive-living, self-control and re-affirmation. Yet it also records the perennial danger of back-sliding and the need for resilience to cope with and prevent regression.

What follows is the record of a very distinct individual who proclaims, and demonstrates, more than mere individuality. His strongest tendency is towards communication, cooperation and the attaining of harmony with other people, the natural world, and that which contains them both.

Ken Burke
March 20, 1978.

Living: A London Journal

10:20 p.m. Tuesday March 23.
I am in the Elbow Room in the Community Centre at the University of Western Ontario in London, Ontario. This is the beginning of my seven day intensive journal. The entertainment is really good. The performer, Jake, is a very good singer and piano player. He just sang "I'd Love to Turn You On" by the Beatles. That song brings back so many memories. He's not getting that good a response. I am one of the few people clapping.

This has been an incredibly good day — one of the best days of my life, one of the happiest and most productive. I'm really happy that I finally got started on this seven day journal book. This is one more area where I am overcoming my tendency to procrastinate. I will write this intensive journal till ten-twenty p.m. next Tuesday, March the thirtieth. I will include the events of today from ten-twenty this morning when Paul Mackenzie called.

I just walked through the Elbow Room and saw Lynn, the waitress here, who is in music at Western. I met her a year ago last October. I had that day just got the idea to do an assemblage (which I called a collage because I thought that was the correct term). I made the assemblage and sold it later on that night to Winston for twenty-five dollars. That day I sat at a table with Lynn and her girlfriend. They were very friendly, so I decided to show them my work of art. They looked at it, went through it, and told me they really liked it. This meant a great deal to me because they were the first people I showed it to, other than my mother.

I hadn't seen Lynn since St. Patrick's Day when I saw her on the bus and said hello. She said hello but wasn't sure I was the person who had showed her the assemblage. I then asked her if she remembered me. She said she did and she then also remembered the assemblage. I told her I had sold it later that night and that I made up and sold several more. Tonight when I saw her she said, "How are you?" I said, "Really good," and sort of nodded towards her; then she bowed towards me and I bowed towards her. That went on for a couple of more bows as we smiled at each other. She is a very beautiful woman about five feet two, with black curly hair, intense green eyes and a good figure. I really like her a lot and want to get to know her better.

As I walked through the Elbow Room, the singer, Jake, said, "Hello Roy how are you?" and shook my hand. I only recognized him then and not when he'd been singing. I told him that he was really good and that I enjoyed his performance very much. I said that the reaction of the audience disturbed me because he was so good and there was very little appreciation. He said, "Oh well this is the Elbow Room." I'd first met him several months ago with Debbie, a woman who works as a waitress at the Bamboo Room in the Ceeps, after a performance of "Death of a Salesman" at Theatre London.

11:20 p.m. Tuesday March 23.
I sat with Debbie and Jake then, as their guest, at the Latin Quarter. It's been a beautiful Spring day all day.

11:30 p.m. Tuesday March 23.
I am on the Richmond bus heading for downtown. I had a coke with a cherry in it in the Elbow Room. The cherry really adds to the flavour. I can still taste it. I saved the cherry for the last as I always do. I paid the waitress, a regular who I find attractive, thirty-five cents for the coke plus a fifteen cent tip. She never even thanked me. That

really annoyed me. Most of the waitresses at the Elbow Room, however, are very friendly.

11:40 p.m. Tuesday March 23.
I'm at the Latin Quarter. As I walked by a group of people, a beautiful woman said hello. I said hello to her but didn't recognize her immediately. She said we talked at the Casino restaurant a few weeks ago. I said, "You're a nurse." She said, "Right." At that time she came up to me and told me that she had met me several years ago at the International Students Club at Western. I vaguely remembered her from the club.

12:05 a.m. Wednesday March 24.
I'm now on the Westminster-Wellington Road bus heading home. I shook hands with the nurse I met. She was wearing her hair in braids and looked really good with long brown hair, clear blue eyes, strong features and a peaches and cream complexion. Also a very good figure. She really turns me on.

12:50 a.m. Wednesday March 24.
I am at home. I just decided that this journal book that I began at ten-twenty p.m. will be a journal of events, feelings, impressions, etc. from ten-twenty p.m. on and not from Tuesday morning because I have much of the day's record down on earlier notes. This way my journal will contain the events of exactly seven days and not eight days.

I find that when I get really self-conscious about this project or keeping my journal in general, the writing doesn't flow properly. It doesn't flow because I get blocked in my self-consciousness and can't write. This journal is a self-portrait in pen and ink. I want people to read this as they would listen to me in person, talking about my life and my reactions to the world around me. I move from subject to subject and story to story, the way I talk, the way most people talk.

Thought about how Paul Mackenzie and I talked Tuesday at our place, in his Volkswagon, at "Mother's" restaurant on Wellington Road and at his place on Askin Street. We hadn't seen each other since October nineteen-seventy-four when he and Niti, his wife, left for Indonesia. He and Niti are only in London for a week. So much to talk about. So little time! I feel that way about this journal. I have so much I want to share of my life with you my reader in so short a time — one week, my self-imposed time limit for writing. Much of the reason for my one week time limit is that I convey in the movement of the book the urgency that I feel about life, time, and communication.

I want to take you with me on a trip through seven days in London. Many times in this book you will be overhearing me as I talk to myself. At other times I will be talking directly to you as though you were a friend of mine. I usually imagine one friend of mine, or another, reading what I've written.

If you are not a friend or even an acquaintance and just happened to be browsing through a book store, glanced at my book, picked it up, read a few passages that you liked and decided to buy the book, then you may come up to me some day at the Latin Quarter, the Ceeps, McDonald's, the London Public Library or another one of my favourite hangouts and say, "Excuse me but didn't you write a book called 'Living: A London Journal'?"

1:30 a.m. Wednesday March 24.
I am at home on Wellington Road. I will then admit to the deed and introduce myself. Hopefully you read the book and liked it. And even if you didn't, we might be able to get a good dialogue going because I love good dialogues. In fact I spend much of my life conversing with people.

When I applied for a Canada Council grant six or seven years ago, I created my own category. I applied as a Free Lance Dialogist. But I didn't get the grant. That happened not too long after the Canada Council got a lot of bad publicity in the papers for giving a grant to Joachim Foikis, Vancouver's Town Fool. As a matter of fact I got into a good dialogue around that time with Foikis who spoke at the Unitarian Fellowship on Victoria Street in London. There we were — Vancouver's Town Fool and London's Free Lance Dialogist!

Back to you my reader. I just want you to know that I am approachable and love meeting people. So if you read this journal and like it, or even don't like it but recognize me and would like to talk with me about the book or about anything else for that matter, come up and say hello.

I just finished off my dinner. Delicious. Scrambled eggs with onions, blue cheese, and pieces of two other kinds of cheese with olives. Then I had a piece of white light cake with vanilla icing and coconut. I don't usually mention in my journals what I ate or how it tasted, yet eating is one of my greatest enjoyments. I never realized this omission till about a year ago when I heard Greg Curnoe read from his journals at the Forest City Gallery on Richmond Street. In several of his journal entries Greg wrote about what he had for breakfast, lunch, and dinner. I had heard him read his journals at the Brescia lecture series four or five years before that, but I couldn't recall him mentioning the food he ate.

1:45 a.m. Wednesday March 24.
While I was at the Latin Quarter earlier I met Maurice, a folk singer who plays there from time to time and also at the Elbow Room. We shook hands. He said that he had seen me around a lot. I then introduced myself to Fern and shook her hand. She said that she had met me about six years ago at Western. I told her that I was sorry but I couldn't place her. She said, "Well you meet a lot of people and I'm not as outgoing as you are." I also met Randell who is in graduate physics at Western. They were all friends of Sandy's, the beautiful nurse.

Saw Mrs. Downs and asked her how she was. She said, "Just fine thank you and how are you Roy?" I said,

"Really good thank you." I sat on a couch where I sat with Sue, the first time I took her out. Jayne was my waitress as I hoped she would be. She asked me how I was. I said I was really feeling good. I asked her if it was all right if I just had a coffee. She smiled, said, "Sure", and touched my hand in the gentle, considerate way she has. I asked her the time and it was 11:45. I paid her right then fifty cents for the coffee and gave her a ten cent tip. I haven't had a coffee in there since I started to drink booze when I was twenty-five.

I order coke, ginger ale or tomato juice since I've stopped drinking. Tea and coffee are the cheapest drinks, so I usually have either one — since I have very little money. Randell sat near me. I asked him the time. After he told me, he mentioned that he had seen me around Western a lot and he asked what I did. I told him that I was a writer, that I had written for various newspapers and magazines across Canada and that now I was writing a book.

2:00 a.m. Wednesday March 24.
I am at home on Wellington Road. Randell said, "What kind of a book?", and I said, "It's a journal about my day-to-day experiences and reflections." I asked him if he had heard of Don Bell but he hadn't. I said that Don wrote a book called "Saturday Night at the Bagel Factory", that won the Stephen Leacock award for humour and that he also wrote for "Weekend Magazine", "Air Canada", and other magazines and newspapers. I told him that Don wrote a fictionalized biography on me called, "Pocketman". I told him the reason I was called "pocketman" was that my pockets, as I showed him, were always full of notebooks, wallets, papers, etc. He said that was a book Sandy should get because she reads a great many books. He said, "She reads everything." He told me what Sandy and Fern did at Western. I told him about Winston's book "Parts of People In These Parts" and a little about some of the people in the book. He was very interested so I gave him an ad for the

book to be put out by Applegarth. He said he would look for the book when it comes out. I told him that it was good meeting him and his friends and that I would see him around. As usual I ran to catch my bus.

I touched one of the two beautiful evergreen trees near the Honeywell building on the corner of Richmond as I ran by. I feel a lot of affection for those two trees. Ran hard for the bus so that I was puffing. Said hello to one of the usual friendly Westminster bus drivers. Said goodnight as I got off the bus. Beautiful starry night. In our backyard I brushed my face against our blue spruce, which is my favourite tree in all the world. Mother was still up reading.

2:30 a.m. Wednesday March 24.
I am at home in my room on Wellington Road. Mother was reading "The Business of Living" by Jack H. Grossman, one of the three books I got Tuesday afternoon at the library when I went there with Mary. Mother also read some of "The Seduction of the Spirit: The Use and Misuse of Peoples' Religion" by Harvey Cox (author of "The Secular City") which she also liked. The third book I got was "Why Our Children Drink" by Edmond G. Addeo and Jovita Reichling Addeo. After I talked to mother for a few minutes I said goodnight, came into my room and did T.M. for twenty minutes. It was good peaceful meditation.

Almost every time I do T.M. at one time or another during the meditation I think of Anne because it was she more than anyone who deepened my involvement with T.M. during the past four months. It was she who convinced me to go for checkings, and the conversations I had with Anne and Doug motivated me to read more about T.M. and get into the movement more deeply.

Paul and I talked about meditation Tuesday afternoon at "Mother's" restaurant. I asked him if he or Niti were doing meditation. He said, "No." He said, "Anne and Doug are really into it aren't they?" I said, "Very much." I said that Anne was a true believer, in a good sense, in T.M. as the hope for humanity. I also think of Anne when I meditate because we have meditated together. I also meditated once with Anne and Doug at Doug's mother's place.

3:30 a.m. Wednesday March 24
At home in my room on Wellington Road. Eating a very tasty orange. Trying to decide what to do on Wednesday, besides keeping this journal of course. Since a week ago last Thursday, every day before I go to bed at night and after I get up in the morning, I engage in some daily planning which takes me about ten minutes. I usually plan to do a task at a certain time or, more accurately, within a certain time span. This planning time I find very valuable. I know that for much of the day I will be writing this intensive journal. I also plan to see Paul and Niti at about nine p.m.

4:00 p.m. Wednesday March 24.
I am at McDonald's drinking a coffee with double cream and no sugar, as usual, which I got from Erin. I asked her how she was. She Said, "Good. How are you?" I said, "Really good." She is on school holidays till Monday because it is spring break. She said, "Roy you're out of breath. Have you been running?" I said, "Oh I run every day for exercise. All year. It's really good for me. It's a beautiful day today." Debbie is here as a customer as are Shirley and Diane and some of the guys who work here. Diane said hello to me and asked how I was. Said hello to Kathy, the brunette, and asked her how she was and said hello to the other Kathy, the beautiful redhead. Kevin, Brenda and Joyce are also working.

After I lay down this morning at about four a.m. I read the first part of "The Business of Living." It's not a great self-help book but it's a good self-help book. The author, Grossman, is a psychologist. His book contains good practical common sense. He makes use of much of the vocabulary of business and applies it to the business of living. I just picked the book up at the library yesterday without doing more than glancing at it briefly. Grossman speaks of the differentiation between those who just exist and those who really live. He speaks of those who go through life just existing, those who do things because not to do them would lead to unpleasant consequences. In the process, they are constantly choosing between the lesser of two evils and life becomes boring drudgery. Those who really live, do things to a great extent because what they do offers them challenge and excitement. They see problems as opportunities for achievement and thus live life with enthusiasm and zest. I basically agree with Grossman's analysis and insights.

After I read I did Zen breath counting for about twenty minutes. Got to sleep around five a.m. Woke up at about nine a.m. and went back to sleep. I got up for the day at about one p.m. when mother called me because father wanted some help. I brushed my face against my favourite tree on my way to the garage; then I went with father to the back shed (which many years ago was our chicken coop, before our property became part of the city of London) to help him fix his wood-burning stove. He had just bought a couple of new stove pipes which we hammered together after fitting them and then screwed them together. He drilled the holes with his Black and Decker electric drill and I put in the screws. At one point a bit earlier as we were working, the pieces of pipe fell apart, fell down, and one of the pieces hit me on the head in the process, leaving a small cut on my forehead and startling me momentarily as the pipe crashed to the floor making a hell of a noise. We didn't get all the work finished because father needed to get another new piece of pipe although he had thought he would be able to use the old piece of stovepipe. Father wants to burn papers and wood in the stove in the late autumn and winter so it will be warm enough out there for him to work, sawing wood with his electric saw.

As I helped him, I repeated to myself affirmations with regard to benefiting from adversity, and affirmations about using time wisely. I repeat these affirmations every day in order to condition my mind to make good use of all that happens to me. This process helps to strengthen me and develops in me a positive mental attitude. After we finished, father thanked me for giving him a hand. I told him he was welcome and that whenever he needed some more help to finish the job after he got the stovepipe, to let me know and I would be glad to help.

4:30 p.m. Wednesday March 24.
I looked through the back shed and the garage as I do from time to time, in order to sharpen my powers of observation and also in order to see these places and their contents clearly in my mind's eye. I also looked at the lawns and trees and houses around our yard. Looked at Small's place behind us on Whetter Ave. and the Polhe's place and the Monroe's. Samuel's book "Seeing With the Mind's Eye," that I got from mother for a Christmas present, is very helpful in terms of helping me to more adequately visualize. Jerome Singer's book "The Inner World of Daydreaming", which I read a couple of months ago, gave me greater insight into the value of visualization to effect beneficial changes in one's life. I hope that book comes out in paperback because I would like to be able to refer to it any time I want to. It is a new hardcover book I borrowed from the library.

After I got in the house, I noticed that I had a cut on my forehead. I mentioned the fact to mother. I didn't intend to bother putting anything on it but mother got out the rubbing alcohol and put some on the cut. I then did T.M. for twenty minutes at about three p.m. because I didn't have the time after I got up. It was a very good peaceful meditation. I had a few short moments when I was simply alert and aware but not thinking about anything. These moments usually only last for a few seconds at a time. Sometimes they last for as long as one or two minutes. I made my usual three just-for-today promises to myself which I make every day without exception and have made for the past four months when I got the idea. I promised myself that just for today I would not drink at all no matter what I felt or what the situation.

4:45 p.m. Wednesday March 24.
I am at McDonald's. I promised myself that just for today I would not allow myself to lose my temper no matter what I felt or what the situation. In addition to these affirmations today I made two new ones: that just for today I would think of the benefits of doing this one week intensive journal for publication and that just for today I would think of the benefits of every other week totally immersing myself in some specific work project. After that I made my daily affirmation for a good day which I have been doing for about two and a half years or about as long as I have been doing T.M. on a reasonably regular basis. I affirm that yesterday was a good day and that today will be as good or better than yesterday, that all my talents and abilities and knowledge will be available to me when I need them to make this a very good, happy, productive day. Then I affirm to myself that I feel happy, I feel healthy, I feel terrific.

When I say that yesterday was a good day or that yesterday was a very good, happy productive day as I often say, I take a few moments to think of the good things that happened yesterday. If the previous day was an unhappy, miserable day, all I say is that yesterday was a good day and that today will be better than yesterday. Then I continue with the rest of the affirmation. I always say that yesterday was a good day — not to fool myself — but to condition myself to realize that even if the day brought a great deal of misery and pain still something good or a few good things — even small ones — happened. Then I spend a little time thinking of these good things.

5:00 p.m. Wednesday March 24.
I am at McDonald's. I affirm that today will be better than yesterday and do my best to make it so. When I say I feel

happy, I feel healthy, I feel terrific, it often sounds like self-mockery because I am saying not what I feel but what I want to feel; but as I say the words, I work at trying to feel what I say I feel. At such times, no matter how miserable I feel or how many things are going wrong, I try to concentrate my attention on the few things that are going right. I also tell myself that things could be one hell of a lot worse. After this last affirmation I am ready for the day's activities. I try to act as though I felt happy, healthy and terrific. These affirmations help me to a considerable extent.

Years ago in a self-help book, I can't remember which one, I read a statement, by an author whose name I don't know, which consisted of several affirmations, each one beginning with the words "Just for today". One of the affirmations read something like this, "Just for today I will be happy, assuming the truth of Abraham Lincoln's statement that 'Most people are just about as happy as they make up their minds to be.' " I had forgotten these just-for-today affirmations when I began to make my own just-for-today promises to myself. I just thought of them now as a matter of fact. Subconsciously, I must have been aware of them — so they may have influenced me.

Much of my own system was inspired by the A.A. programme of living one day at a time without alcohol. I started out with the affirmation with regards to not drinking a few days after I had my last drink on November twenty-second, nineteen-seventy-five. The affirmation really helped me to go on the wagon.

5:30 p.m. Wednesday March 24.
I am at McDonald's on Wellington Road. David, my friend in A.A. in Montreal, several times talked to me about the A.A. members' use of the affirmation that they wouldn't drink today, actually that today they would refuse their first drink. David makes this affirmation to himself every morning. With regards to my affirmation about not losing my temper, it helps me because it comes to mind very

often when I am in a situation that could easily lead to loss of temper. I have not fully lost my temper since September the thirteenth, nineteen-seventy-five. The last time I halfway lost my temper was last November. Today is exactly three months since I decided that I didn't intend to allow myself to lose my temper ever again. I can't say that I will never lose my temper again, only that I never intend to. I don't want to ever again lose my temper. Keeping my temper one day at a time is my goal. I feel that I can control my temper at least for twenty-four hours at a time. When I start to get depressed, I think of my affirmation about depression and really work at getting rid of my depressed feelings so that they don't drag me down into a state which is very hard to get out of.

6:30 p.m. Wednesday March 24.
I am at the Country Style Donuts shop on Wellington Road. Debbie was the hostess looking after childrens' birthday parties at McDonald's when a group of kids came in with a couple of adults to celebrate a birthday. I told Debbie that I would move for them; then I said I would leave since I had been there long enough. The place was packed and there were lineups from the counter to the tables. I said to Debbie, "You're on school holidays eh?" She said, "Yeah, just for a week." She thanked me for giving the kids my place and gave me one of her angelic smiles that always makes me feel good. With her clear light blue eyes and her honey blond hair, she looks as beautiful as she is.

When I left McDonald's, I ran up here. I ran for the exercise and to save time. I did a Psychosynthesis meditation on the body. Today is one of the first times in several months that I didn't get my coffee refill at McDonald's. I had a turtle candy before I left home. That's all I have eaten today. Turtles are without a doubt my favourite candy.

6:45 p.m. Wednesday March 24.
I am at the Country Style Donuts shop on Wellington Road drinking a small chocolate milk that cost twenty-five cents, which I got from May. I said, "Hello. Beautiful day isn't it?" She said, "Yes it's really lovely and what would you like today, a small coke or a small 7-Up?" I usually have one or the other but I want to get into the habit of drinking milk here, rather than coke, or 7-Up, or coffee. I drink too much coffee and coke as the price I pay for admission to bars and restaurants.

Lu, the other waitress just came in to work. She said, "How are you Roy?" I said, "Good and how are you?" I said, "You know my name but I don't know yours." She said, "It's Lu." I said, "Is that short for Louise?" She said, "No it's short for Lulu."

She hadn't called me by name before or asked me how I was, so I found it pleasant when she did so. She is a pleasant, attractive woman in her thirties, I believe. Bill, the taxi driver, is here as are several of the other regulars. Bill said hello when I came in.

7:45 p.m. Wednesday March 24.
I'm at home. I paid Lu twenty-five cents and she gave me back a nickel. I said, "No I owe you twenty-five cents." She said, "What did you have?" I said, "A small chocolate milk." She said, "I'm so used to you ordering a small coke I just assumed that's what you had." She certainly has a good memory for what customers order. I said goodbye to Bill and Lisa's (the girl who goes to South who used to work at the Country Style Donuts shop) boyfriend. Bill said, "Where are you heading now, McDonald's?"

I said, "No I was just there. I guess I'll go to the Latin Quarter later on."

Bill said, "I thought you were on the wagon." I said, "I am but I still go to pubs like the Latin Quarter and the Ceeps that I used to go to." Bill said, "I could never do that." I said, "Why not?" Lisa's boyfriend said, "Because Bill doesn't have the willpower not to drink."

I said, "I'm an alcoholic so I can't afford to drink at all."

As I ran home I thought about the fact that I have been in a hurry for most of my life. I have always liked to circulate around a lot from place to place, bar to bar, restaurant to restaurant. When I was younger, I liked to go from church to church and from one young peoples' group to another. At one time I was a member of several young peoples' groups. I was a member of the High C group at Metropolitan United Church, Young Peoples' at Central Baptist, Calvary United Church Young Peoples', St. James' Anglican Church Anglican Young Peoples' Association, and Wesley United Church Young Peoples'. I was also in Kairos, the United Church young adults. Those were very good days and worthwhile church groups. Happy memories.

I read in The Toronto Star tonight at the donut shop that an independent research group has predicted that by this Sunday there will be four billion people on earth. One billion people have been added in the last fifteen years. This is incredible but a danger sign. It certainly isn't any occasion for rejoicing. It should be a day of mourning and deep soul-searching on behalf of the family of man. What Paul Mackenzie and people like him are doing all over the world to limit population growth through education and family planning clinics is extremely important to the peace and well-being of mankind.

8:30 p.m. Wednesday March 24.
I am at home on Wellington Road. I just ate some dinner, pumpkin pie with buttermilk, which was delicious, and also a few grapes. I read in The Toronto Star where the Young Progressive Conservatives have advocated that the government ban liquor advertising from radio and T.V. They mentioned the irresponsibility of companies who advertise alcoholic beverages in such a way that their use is seen as being synonymous with a happy social life. They also believe the law should penalize bars where people don't have to show identification as proof of legal

age to get in. I agree with their position on identity checks but don't believe they go far enough with respect to advertising. I would like to see alcohol advertising phased out completely. Society is finally moving in the right direction towards more control of the approaches advertisers are allowed to use. I agree with the ban on cigarette advertising on radio and T.V. I want to see this happen with alcohol as well. I also want to see alcohol and cigarette advertising banned from newspapers, magazines, and billboards. This is one hell of a fight that must be waged against the vested interests of multi-million-dollar companies with enormous lobbying power.

11:40 p.m. Wednesday March 24.
I am at McDonald's on Wellington Road, drinking my second coffee that I got from Diana. I just shook hands and said goodbye to Paul and wished him well. Paul and I got here at about ten p.m. Lorri the pretty, vivacious brunette — who reminds me of one of the leads in American Grafitti — served us. I said, "How are you?" She said, "Fine how are you?" I said, "Really good." I also said hello to Theresa and asked her how she was.

I told Paul that I come here twice a day. He said, "The waitresses here must know you really well then." I said, "They do and I really enjoy coming here because of that." I said that most of the waitresses are young and very attractive. At about seven-thirty I called Winston to invite him to have coffee at our place with Paul and Niti but he wasn't home. Later I called up Judy to ask her how she was and how her new job at McCormick's was working out. She said the work wasn't strenuous but just really boring. I said that kind of work would really infuriate me because I would feel that my employers were robbing me of my time. Judy feels much the same way I do about that kind of job. She wants to go back to school in the fall so she is just working for the money. She wants to take a college psychology programme but doesn't like Western's emphasis on behaviourism. I mentioned to Judy the article I had skimmed through yesterday at the library in "Horizon" magazine, on behaviourism. She hadn't heard of the magazine so I told her about it and its high quality. I told her about the wide variety of excellent articles in the magazine and the quality art reproductions. She said she'd like to read the article on behaviourism.

11:55 p.m. Wednesday March 24.
I'm at McDonald's. There was a programme on the radio called "Concern" that I listened to for the first time tonight. The programme dealt with suicide in children and teenagers. They stated on the programme that suicide was the second highest cause of the death of adolescents, the first cause being automobile accidents. People who had made suicide attempts were talking on the programme. Suicide notes were read.

Paul came around at about nine-fifteen p.m. My parents, Paul, and I listened to the programme till it ended at nine-thirty. I told Paul I was very interested in the subject partly because of Rose's death and the death of other good friends of mine by suicide. The programme emphasized that suicide attempts were usually calls for help. The commentators stressed lack of communication in the family and the breakdown of the family as a very important factor leading to suicide. They spoke of the lack of stability in terms of peoples' lifestyles and the fact that many people aren't aware of having an identity. The commentators stated that the suicide by his or her act is establishing an identity. They said the suicide is saying, "See! I have an identity. I am a suicide!" However, the suicide isn't around to realize his identity. People on the programme who had attempted suicide talked about their use of drugs, about breakups of love affairs and about their parents not caring about them. The programme made me very angry as I related Rose's suicide and the suicide of other friends of mine to what was said. I thought about the things that people on the programme said about attempting suicide and these things reminded me a lot of the situations and reasons that had nearly driven me to kill myself. Now I am very, very glad to be alive. Then I felt the future was hopeless and that I would never get out of my depression.

12:30 a.m. Thursday March 25.
I am at McDonald's which is staying open till one a.m. this morning because it is a school holiday. The guy who was cleaning up told me that McDonald's stayed open till one a.m. every night last summer.

My parents were glad to see Paul as they always are. I asked Paul if he would like a coffee at our place but he suggested that we go out, so I suggested McDonald's. My mother said, "Well I guess we won't be seeing you for a while." He said, "Probably not for a year and a half." He gets vacation time every eighteen months. Paul told me on Tuesday that he would like me to suggest to him a list of books that he should get and send to Nigeria, his next posting. I said I would. I told him at that time about the book "Psychosynthesis" by Roberto Assagioli. He wrote down the title and at that point Mary came around.

1:15 a.m. Thursday March 25.
I am at home on Wellington Road. As I wrote the above about Paul at McDonald's, Ken, one of the managers, came around and sat down at my table. He said, "I see you're getting a lot of work done." I said, "Yes my writing is going well." I told him that I had just said goodbye to a very good friend who I probably wouldn't see for another year and a half. He said he saw me come in with Paul. I mentioned that Paul spent the last year and a half in Indonesia, and previously had been in Tanzania for a couple of years. I said Paul had spent time on all the continents.

Ken said he had been in the States a few times and had been around Canada some but hadn't done much travelling at all. He told me about a friend of his in his twenties who had been around the world twice and was knowledgeable about a lot of it. I said Paul was that way. Bill, another manager, came and sat down. We talked about hockey. He mentioned how well Montreal was doing in the series but that they lost the game he just watched, to the Toronto Maple Leafs I believe. I told him I had never been anywhere where people had anywhere near as much enthusiasm for hockey as they do in Montreal.

I mentioned watching a playoff game in the Montreal Forum when Montreal started out two to nothing and ended up winning the game. I said every time a Montreal player scored, the fans would jump to their feet, clap, yell, and cheer so loud it was deafening. I said I had to hold my ears. He said at the game he watched in the Forum, some of the Montreal fans were actually booing their players till they started scoring and then they yelled and cheered, hoping their team would come from behind and win. But they lost. I said that I spent a lot of time in Montreal and that when Montreal was in the playoffs, bars and restaurants all over bring in portable T.V. sets which nearly everyone watches. He was in the Forum once and really liked it. He said Maple Leaf Gardens in Toronto is really poor in comparison. I was only at a hockey game once in Toronto about nineteen years ago when I was at the Ontario Older Boy's Parliament in the Ontario Legislature during Christmas vacation. At that time, Toronto was playing Montreal. Maurice (Rocket) Richard, my hockey hero then, was attempting to score his five-hundredth goal but he didn't in that game. It was a really good game and the first professional hockey game I had ever seen. I forget which team won. The only other professional hockey game I have ever seen live was the one I just mentioned in the Montreal Forum about three or four years ago. I have always enjoyed playing hockey and watching hockey.

1:30 a.m. Thursday March 25.
I am at home. I can remember back when I was a little kid

and listened to Foster Hewitt, the sportscaster, give his play by play descriptions on Hockey Night In Canada. My grandfather used to listen to the hockey broadcast every Saturday night during the season. Maybe I get my interest from him originally, although I don't know because I was only about four or five when he died. I can still remember sitting on his lap while he read childrens' books to me. Grandpa Goodwin, mother's father, meant a lot to me and was really good to me.

1:45 a.m. Thursday March 25.
I am at home on Wellington Road. I just finished a piece of very tasty coconut pastry and another small piece of cake. When Paul came over here at nine-fifteen p.m. on Wednesday I invited him into my room — office — studio, for it is all three, to look at some of my books. I showed him "Psychosynthesis" by Assagioli. He had looked for it downtown but couldn't find it. I showed him "Powers of Mind" by Adam Smith which I highly recommended. I said that the author had been a participant in the various workshops for the expansion of consciousness that he wrote about. I said he was very knowledgeable and very easy to read. Paul had read "T.M. Discovering Inner Energy and Overcoming Stress" which I showed him. I said it was the best book I had read on T.M. I recommended "How to Meditate" by Lawrence LeShan which he looked at. I also recommended "The Medium, The Mystic and the Physicist: Toward a General Theory of the Paranormal" by the same author. I said that in the book, LeShan was illustrating how many of the theoretical speculations of modern physicists tie in with insights in the area of parapsychology. I first read a selection from LeShan's book "The Medium, The Mystic and the Physicist" that was just coming out, about a year and a half or two years ago in "Intellectual Digest" when I was in Montreal.

I showed Paul my library copy of "The Seduction of the Spirit: The Use and Misuse of People's Religion" by Harvey Cox. I said it looked like a good book but that I hadn't gotten into it yet. I recommended highly "Frontiers of Consciousness", a source book of perspectives on Noetics, which is the study of man's consciousness, edited by John White. I said that "The New Psychotherapies" by Robert Harper provides a very good, unbiased assessment of new developments in the field of psychotherapy. I showed Paul "Awakening" by William Henderson, subtitled "Ways To Psycho-Spiritual Growth". I said the book provides a good, well balanced assessment of various schools and societies that lead their students and members to self-realization.

I showed him "To A Dancing God" by Sam Keen. Told Paul how much I liked Keen's thinking and his writing style and mentioned a bit about Keen's background including the fact that he did interviews for "Psychology Today". I highly recommended "Peace Making: A Guide to Conflict Resolution", a book of readings by a good variety of experts in the field from Ruth Benedict to Martin Luther King Jr. I said that "Exploring the Crack in the Cosmic Egg" by Joseph Chilton Pearce was a fascinating book. He said that a few hours before he had bought "The Crack in the Cosmic Egg". Talked a bit about the difference between the two books by Pearce. He looked through "In The Garden: Murshid Sam". I said that it was a really good book on Sam a Sufi. Paul wanted to know if Sufism was spreading over here. I said that there is a growing interest in the movement and philosophy. Told Paul that Mary gave me the book for Christmas but that I hadn't heard of it before then.

2:15 a.m. Thursday March 25.
I am at home on Wellington Road. I showed Paul the manuscript of "Pocketman", Don Bell's book on me. I gave him the section to read where Don included a quote from "Sexus" by Henry Miller that Paul quoted in a letter to me several years ago from Tanzania. Paul remembered the letter. Don Bell also quoted some of Paul's poem to me on my thirtieth birthday. This Paul also recalled. I then had

him read the passage entitled "Go West Young Man" which was about me getting a two month Ameripass with the two hundred dollars Paul gave me before he and Niti left for Indonesia, on which for the two months all I did was make my usual round trips between London and Montreal, only once extending my route by going to Quebec City. The pass was good for two months of unlimited travel all over the U.S. and Canada. Paul smiled as he read it and laughed a couple of times, so I believe he enjoyed it. At least I hope he did. I said that what he read was a good section but not anywhere near Don's best. I wanted him to read the section about Don, Carolyn, and I and her shih tzu dog in the adult education English class at Dawson College in Montreal but he didn't want to take the time. He said, "I'll read it all someday when it gets published."

I said Don is changing the book a considerable amount at the present time so that the "Pocketman" manuscript I have will be very different from the new, considerably improved, soon-to-be-completed version. As we were leaving I showed Paul the book "Seeing With the Mind's Eye" by Mike and Nancy Samuels. I mentioned that Mike was a doctor and a photographer. I said they spent several years building their own house. Paul looked through the book and found it interesting. I said the book was a favourite of mine. I asked Paul if he had met Ken Burke. I wasn't sure if he had or not. He seemed to recall someone by that name yet couldn't recall for sure.

2:45 a.m. Thursday March 25.
I am in my room on Wellington Road. I turned on my tape recorder to the conversation that Ken and I had which was one of our dialogue series. He didn't recall the voice. I told Paul that I have always loved a good conversation and that what I want to do is to have a series of dialogues with various friends of mine and transcribe the dialogues into a book. I said I would like to have a dialogue with him in the book and a dialogue with Greg Curnoe and several others.

I said I realized not too long ago that all my good friends are good conversationalists. I mentioned some of the great conversations we have had over the years in the areas of psychology, philosophy, theology, and in many other areas. On our way to McDonald's Paul mentioned how much he enjoyed our discussions because we share so many similar concerns. We had a very good discussion at McDonalds although it only lasted for an hour and a half. Lorri waited on us. When she came to me she said, "I know you want coffee with double cream." I said, "Yes please." Paul had a hot chocolate. I offered to pay but he insisted on paying.

4:00 a.m. Thursday March 25.
I am at home on Wellington Road. My fingers are getting tired from all the writing I have been doing today and yesterday. I didn't record any of the dreams I had last night because I only remembered bits and pieces of dreams and they were very jumbled and didn't make sense. I do remember a feeling of urgency in my dream state, a feeling that I had to get twice as much accomplished in my daily activities as I usually do. This is a carry-over from my waking thoughts about my alternate week, total immersion, method of work. I am now engaging in planning time, trying to figure out what I will do when I get up. I want to visit Western University. I intend to keep up this intensive journal of course.

2:00 p.m. Thursday March 25.
I am at McDonald's on Wellington Road, drinking a coffee I got from Lorri the pretty blue eyed brunette. I said, "Hello, how are you, beautiful day isn't it?" She said, "I'm fine thank you; yes it really is nice out." She knew what I wanted of course but she also gave me two sugars which she thought I took. I took the sugar to give to mother. I never take sugar in tea or coffee — never have for that matter except for an occasional time that I take it for variety. I always drink coffee and tea with double cream or

lots of milk. I drink it that way for the taste. I have drunk black coffee very few times, for variety, or because there didn't happen to be any cream or milk around. I also take the cream or milk for the food value. I really like café au lait. Half coffee and half milk is ideal for me. The cream also has a buffering effect on the action of the caffeine. I said hello to Lori the attractive, friendly, redhead and Shirley, the very good looking blue-eyed blonde with long wavy hair. Debbie is also working.

I went to bed at about four-thirty this morning but I was still keyed up because of all the concentrated writing I did. Mother called me at ten as I asked her to but I was too tired to get up. I finally got up at eleven when mother called me to tell me that father wanted some help.

Last night when Paul and I were here he got to talking about the merits of oriental women as opposed to occidental women in terms of attractiveness. He feels that Asian women are more attractive on the whole than Western women and that very few of them are homely as a lot of women are over here. On the other hand, he finds very few really beautiful Asian women but quite a few really beautiful Western women. Westerners have a far greater degree of variety in appearance. As for myself, I prefer the wide variety of appearance.

Paul didn't feel that he got much accomplished in Indonesia. He was in charge of an experimental project involving about half-a-million people. The project was to integrate family planning with total health care in the community. I said the concept was certainly sound. He agreed but then mentioned the problems he encountered.

After he completes his year and a half in Nigeria, he said he wanted to sit back for a year or so at his home on Askin Street, in London, and read all the books he's wanted to read for so long and to do some introspection. When Paul says he has accomplished very little, I tend to take what he says with a grain of salt because he is as a rule overly modest and tends to under-rate his achievements.

He felt he was accomplishing something when he was practicing medicine. Then he could see the results of his work in front of him. He also felt he was accomplishing something when he was teaching because he was passing on knowledge which was needed. Paul said he is just beginning to realize how very big the world is and how little one person can do. He said, "One person can't do very much." I said, "Yes but one person can do something to better the world and that's the important thing. One has to keep fighting." I said that while I was involved with Friends of the Student Non-Violent Coordinating Committee in Canada, (The Canadian group that supported the U.S. Student Non-Violent Coordinating Committee) and when I was involved in protests, marches and Teach-Ins concerning the war in Vietnam, a lot of people — a hell of a lot of people — didn't join in support of the movement which they believed in, using as an excuse the fact that one person didn't matter much.

2:30 p.m. Thursday March 25.
I am at McDonald's on Wellington Road. I said that much of the problem with the world today is that people tend to feel that they don't matter, that what they do or don't do isn't important. People feel that they can't change anything so they don't try. Paul said, "I guess you're right." I recommended to Paul that he read "More Power Than We Know" by Dave Dellinger. I mentioned Dellinger's long involvement with civil rights and protests against the American involvement in the Vietnam war, and his non-violence position. I said that I agreed with Dellinger's position entirely, which is that one needs to be involved with the religious and spiritual aspects of life in terms of seeking enlightment and greater awareness but also one should express this greater awareness in social and political action for the betterment of society. Dellinger writes of the danger of people seeking their own enlightenment and at the same time not seeing themselves as a part of a social and political movement seeking

the betterment of society. Dellinger stresses the danger of ignoring the religious dimension, the spiritual dimension and concentrating on the "correct", Communist, Marxist, Leninist, Trotskyist, etc. line for bringing about social change. This kind of doctrinaire materialism leads to oppression and inhumane treatment of human beings in the name of freedom and equality. One needs to explore, develop and make full use of the inner world and the outer world. Dellinger also spoke of and emphasized the importance of radical anti-Capitalist anti-war groups living the revolution, in that they embody in their own life styles and relations with others the values they hope to see realized in society.

3:00 p.m. Thursday March 25.
At McDonald's on Wellington Road, drinking a coffee. I told Paul that I have always been as interested in developing my own awareness and consciousness as I have been in social action and that I have felt for a long time that the two go together. Paul mentioned that he had a good talk with Barry the other day. He said Barry was really involved in Gurdjieff's philosophy and has been for over a year. I found this very surprising. When Paul called me last Sunday I told him that I had seen Barry a few months ago at an art show opening at the London Public Library. I said I didn't recognize him till he spoke to me because I hadn't seen him for years and he looked a lot older. I said his gray hair really surprised me. He now has two children and is doing well according to Paul. I asked Paul if he had heard about the report of an independent research group that has predicted that by this Sunday the earth will have four billion people on it. He said he hadn't heard about the report and thought there were already more than four billion people on earth. He said that the earth's population will reach six billion by the year two-thousand and there's nothing we can do about it, because of the people already alive. He said that at this point most countries and most people realize the importance of population planning and

population control. He said there isn't much opposition outside of the Roman Catholic Church for such programmes. He also said that most countries realize the importance of government support for such programmes. Paul forsees widespread famine in poor underdeveloped countries in the not too distant future, in this century at least. He said that as usual the poor, the have nots, get hit the hardest. He believes that because of many factors, population stability being one of them, we in North America can afford the luxury of consciousness expansion because we have the time for it.

3:30 p.m. Thursday March 25.
I am at McDonald's on Wellington Road. Paul asked me about what I saw ahead for North America. I mentioned that a great many people are getting into consciousness expanding activities of all kinds that lead to the development of one's potential and increase awareness. I said I believed that on the whole the trend was beneficial.

3:45 p.m. Thursday March 25.
At McDonald's on Wellington Road. I just got a second coffee from Lori, the redhead. I said, "You're still on school holidays eh?" She said, "Yes fortunately till Monday. Beautiful day out isn't it?" I agreed that it was a great day.

Saw Kathy, the brunette, and said, "Hello Kathy how are you?" She said, "Oh surviving I guess." She always says something like that. Kathy, Lori's sister, is also working now. Said hello to Brenda. She said, "Hello Roy how are you today?" I said, "Just great." There have been a lot of people come in since I got here, mostly children and teenagers. I noticed one girl sitting with a group near me. She had bright blue eyes, short dark brown hair, a wide expressive mouth and very delicate features. I kept looking at her from time to time, then looking away so that she wouldn't think I was staring at her. She looked at me a few times. She had a radiant smile. She is a little beauty and in a few years she will be a knockout. I hated to see her leave.

7:30 p.m. Thursday March 25
I'm on the Richmond bus for downtown, going to the new Smales Pace coffee house. Tonight is the opening. I ran home from McDonald's at four-thirty p.m. Father asked me to help him. He wanted to put some caulking cement on the roof of the back shed to seal the area around the chimney so water wouldn't come in and rust the new stove pipes he got. I carried out the aluminum extension ladder and did the job. He needed to do very little. While helping father I went through a Psychosynthesis meditation on feelings.

On my way home a guy with a beard in a truck motioned me over to the side of the truck. I thought it was either someone I knew or someone who wanted directions. He offered me a ride because he saw me heading somewhere fast. I introduced myself to him, shook hands, and thanked him but told him that I was just running for the exercise and that I lived a few doors down. His attitude towards being helpful reminded me of the beneficial aspect of the hippie movement. People like him did that kind of thing for people very frequently back in the late sixties. When it happens nowadays, it's a pleasant surprise.

Mother told me when I got in the house that Gordon had called. He was the guy I met at the opening a week ago at the McIntosh Gallery of Southern Exposure, where I saw the photographs taken in Mexico by Fanshawe students. Gordon wants to photograph me. He told mother he would call me at seven but I waited till seven twenty-five and he hadn't called. I am really looking forward to him photographing me because of the high quality of his work that I saw in the show. I ate some chocolate ice cream with corn syrup which is a tasty combination; then I ate a mincemeat tart. I lay down and slept from five-fifteen to seven. I suddenly realized that the new Smales Pace is opening tonight. A few days ago mother showed me a piece in a local paper that comes around free about the Smales Pace opening. I almost forgot about the opening. I was at the original Smales Pace on Clarence Street at its opening.

8:10 p.m. Thursday March 25.
I am sitting at a table in Smales Pace on Talbot Street. On my way here I saw Mary, the daughter of the woman who owned Smales Pace for its last couple of years. I can't think of her name but I know it. Roberto Assagioli would probably say that the name was in my middle unconscious. I just realized that it's been several months since I have used the two basic Psychosynthesis diagrams as aids to meditation. Now that I realize this I will use them again. This place looks good but because of the shape of the room and its interior it doesn't have nearly as homey an atmosphere as the original. Here there is a big long rectangular room that seats over one hundred people. It is well decorated with original furnishings from the other coffee house. Wednesday night will be a hootenanny night. People are invited then to come and jam or sing or recite poetry. Admission Wednesday is fifty cents. Thursday to Sunday nights the coffee house is open from eight-thirty on and costs two-fifty admission. Mary, the daughter of the former owner of the original Smales Pace, just heard about the opening night. She told me that her mother and a friend, who helped run the original Smales Pace, have opened up a fishing lodge up north. Mary is living near Galt. I told her that when she talked to her mother or wrote to her to tell her hello for me.

There was a reasonably long lineup of people waiting for the doors to open at eight p.m. They are playing a Willie P. Bennett record or tape. I just introduced myself and shook hands with Phylis my waitress, a very pretty blue eyed honey blonde about sixteen who is really friendly. I asked her if she had been a waitress at the other Smales but she said she hadn't. Only one girl waitressing here tonight had been a waitress there. I told her she looked familiar and that I had seen her around. She thought she had seen me around. Told her it was good meeting her.

8:25 p.m. Thursday March 25.
I am at Smales Pace on Talbot Street between York and King. The place is now packed, which is great. London very much needs a good coffee house. The other Smales Pace closed at the end of last August. I was there at the closing. I have spent a lot of time in every coffee house London has ever had. I went to the Jolly Coachman on King Street near Adelaide right from the time it first opened. I am going into a nostalgia trip with regards to coffee houses I have been in.

8:35 p.m. Thursday March 25.
At Smales Pace on Talbot Street. Drinking a special coffee, called borge, recommended to me by the waitress. It consists of coffee, cinnamon, whipped-cream and chocolate and costs forty cents. A very tasty concoction. I have always loved coffee houses and I get off on the kind of people who frequent them. Doug McArthur is playing tonight. Coming in, I said hello to Stan Rogers. Tonight the show is on CFPL radio F.M. The announcer said the "biggies" will be playing here. He said he got a call tonight from Chris Kearney who will be playing here soon. I clapped for that because Chris is an old friend of mine from the Yellow Door Coffee House and the Back Door Coffee House in Montreal. A few years ago, in Montreal, Chris had me on his F.M. radio show. On the show I recited poetry and talked about free schools, especially about my experiences as a paid resource person during the first months of Rochdale College in Toronto. On the programme, I read "Driveway Death Knell" by Jim Schaefer who wrote the poem about the death of my old black Volkswagon, that died in the driveway of Barb's home. I also recited some of my own poetry. I remember hearing

Chris at Café André in Montreal the night I treated Alice and Wavell to the performance. Chris mentioned that he was doing a request for an old friend of his from London, Ontario, who every now and then hitches into town or comes in by Greyhound. The last time I talked to Chris was last summer when he performed at the Home County Folk Festival in Victoria park. I took Linda to the festival on the first afternoon. I was going to introduce her to Chris because she enjoyed his music but when I talked to him she was busy.

9:20 p.m. Thursday March 25.
At Smales Pace. Doug McArthur is very good. He is displaying a good sense of humour in his stage manner which is an important asset to a performer. Many of the songs he sings are his own. The audience here tonight is ideal — quiet, attentive, and very appreciative.

I just realized that three months ago today, Christmas Day, I made up my mind not to ever again allow myself to get into a state of depression. My last severe depression was last September from September thirteenth to the eighteenth. I realize that I can't afford to let the depressed moods, that I get from time to time, drag me down. I have to work very hard to fight off these feelings of depression. With me, depression often leads to drinking, getting drunk and losing my temper and raging. I have to catch myself when I start to go into a down mood. When I get down too far, it's hard as hell to shake off the depression.

Back to the present scene. I like a lot of Doug's songs, especially the train song, "Linda's Got the Blues Again", which he just sang. For a long time I have wanted to write songs but as yet have never written a single song. I intend to write some song lyrics but I don't know enough about music to be able to set my songs to music. I want to write folk songs most of all. I certainly have an abundance of material from life experiences to write folk songs about. I just told Doug that I really enjoyed his performance. He thanked me. Stan Rogers is starting the next set.

10:00 p.m. Thursday March 25.
At Smales Pace. I am really getting off on sitting back and digging the atmosphere and the people here. There is a beautiful blue-eyed woman about twenty, with a friendly look, who smiles at me from time to time, sitting across the table. When I first saw her she reminded me of Anne. I thought of the many times I went to the Jolly Coachman Coffee House with Anne and Doug. Most of all I remember the time when I was twenty-four being there with Sally, Anne and Doug. Anne and Doug borrowed my car to go and see Charlie Savage and Sally and I walked back to Anne and Doug's place where she was staying. Sally and I had a good talk and a beautiful time together. That was a very happy day, one of the happiest days of my life. Sally is someone I would like very much to see again. A coffee-house atmosphere always spurs my imagination and my nostalgic feelings as well.

10:20 p.m. Thursday March 25.
I have been doing my intensive journal for two full days now. Only five days to go. I feel good about what I am doing. I am doing what I generally do from day to day, the only difference is that I am spending more of my time writing my journal record than I usually do, although there have been days when I have written as much or more than I have written on each of these last two days.

There are a lot of beautiful women around here. I always feel better and more creative with beautiful women around.

During these past two days I have pushed myself as hard as I could. I have lived with great intensity as well as written this journal with as much intensity as possible. I am facing the same problem I have always faced in terms of writing my journal. When I live with great intensity I don't have that much time to record my experiences in this ongoing record. During the last two days I have been so busy doing other work, conversing with people and reading that I haven't been able to record my experiences, feelings, thoughts and sensations in as much detail as I would have liked to have done. Many things that I would really like to record I can't record at all because of the time factor.

There is also the problem of style that I have always faced with regard to my journals. I try to get down notes on my experiences, thoughts, and feelings as soon as possible after they occur, usually within minutes or hours. I need to get the notes down quickly because my emotional set and physical setting is always changing. These are journal sketches and impressions and, as such, are not open to revision, or at least I don't feel right about doing revisions of my journals. If I spent more time working on writing what I have to say in a better, more literary style, I wouldn't be able to record my experiences in nearly as much detail as I now record them. Also I wouldn't be able to record a quarter of the experiences I now record.

I try to write as clearly and lucidly and as well as possible within the limitations I have set myself. I find that at such times when I become overly concerned with style, my writing starts to look forced and artificial. Spontaneity, feeling, directness and a sense of movement are the qualities that are most important to me in my writing.

11:15 p.m. Thursday March 25.
At Smales Pace listening to Doug McArthur do his second set. Stan Rogers just played a few songs and was really good. I have always enjoyed his playing and singing.

These journals are the attempt of one individual, myself, to document his experiences, sensations, feelings, imaginings, desires, thoughts, and intuitions as he lives as fully as possible his day to day existence.

I have kept a journal off and on since I was thirteen when my mother gave me a small, black, five by seven inch diary for Christmas. I was fascinated by the idea that a person could record what happened to him every day in such a book, and then, years later, be able to look back and read about what happened to him on a certain date.

When I was sixteen I wrote a travel diary of a trip my parents, a cousin, and I took out to Saskatchewan to visit my aunt, uncle, and cousins. Since I was eighteen, I have kept a journal with as much regularity as possible.

I consider this journal, this record I have kept with regularity for twenty years, to be my life work. I am a diarist by vocation.

12:05 a.m. Friday March 26.
I'm now on the Westminster bus heading for McDonald's. I decided to leave even though, since it was opening night, they were going to have one more set. The beautiful waitress I met who I thought was sixteen is in grade thirteen at Clarke Road high school, so she's probably eighteen but she can't be any older than that. As I left she said it was good meeting me and talking to me. Her saying that really made me feel good. Several people said goodnight to me. I spoke to Walter Grasser briefly. It was an excellent opening. There was a very good feeling at Smales Pace that I hope will continue to be there.

Now I'm at McDonald's. The girl who served me said, "How are you tonight?" I said, "Really good. I was just at the opening of a new coffee house." Theresa said hello. It's a very quiet night here. I intend to go to the new Smales Pace once a week while I am in London.

12:20 a.m. Friday March 26.
At McDonald's on Wellington Road. I am engaging in planning time, trying to figure out what I will do after I get up this morning. I want to go to Western. I thought today about the fact that with my alternate-week total-immersion work project schedule I will be able, after I do one week of total-immersion work, to begin my next immersion week after one week or less. I will do at least one week of immersion work every fortnight and I will always do it seven days in a row in order to keep up my momentum and my concentration. I may decide to begin my next concentrated work week within two or three or

four days rather than one full week after my last work week. What is essential is that I always do one total-immersion work week every fourteen days. This work plan is very important to me as a way of imposing discipline on myself. The plan is realistic, flexible, and not overly ambitious. The plan is ideal in that the immersion in my project gets me fully involved and helps me to push myself as hard as possible for a reasonable length of time — seven days; then it allows me to relax completely for up to a week and do whatever appeals to me at the time. I have the advantage of up to a week of completely free, unstructured time, along with a week of highly-structured time.

My previous work schedules were not successful for me because they involved steady application and hard work for too long a period of time. I would create a far too ambitious work schedule, then give it up soon after I started because it was too exhausting. My present plan is unique and perfect for my needs and personality. I just got a second coffee from Theresa and asked her if she liked folk music. I told her about the Smales Pace opening. I mentioned to her that I wrote poetry and recited poetry at coffee houses. I said I recited my own poetry as well as the poetry of Shakespeare, Keats, Blake, Dylan Thomas, Bob Dylan and others. She was interested in the fact that I wrote poetry. I just bought an apple pie to take home to my parents.

1:30 a.m. Friday March 26.

I am at the Country Style Donuts shop on Wellington Road, drinking a small coke. Bev is the all night waitress. I tell her I have been in often but haven't seen her for a while. She is working part time. Anne — the friendly, attractive, buxom blue-eyed blonde — is here. I say hello to her. She says, "Hello, how are you?" and gives me a pleasant smile.

I feel really good knowing that I have finally, at thirty-eight, developed a work plan that suits me perfectly. This work plan will greatly increase my productivity in the coming years. What is all important is that I push myself to the limits of my ability for seven days in a row once every two weeks. I thought about the Transactional Analysis procedure that involves making a contract with oneself as a means of bringing about a desired behaviour change. I just thought of calling my plan my Fortnightly Schedule. I need to make a contract with myself that I will faithfully keep my schedule. I decided earlier in the week that I intend to keep my fortnightly schedule for the rest of my life. I started my first such schedule Tuesday night at Western.

I know that I can totally immerse myself in a work project of my own choice for one week at a time. At the beginning of my seven day work schedule I always need to make a contract with myself, that regardless of what happens, short of an emergency, I will put in seven days of concentrated work. I know that I can persist in my chosen work project for at least seven days. I just decided that each fortnight I will work exactly seven days in a row, no more and no less. I will finish my work project on the same day of the week, the same hour and minute I started at. With this system, I know exactly how much time I have left to finish my project. I know how many days have gone by and how many days I have to go. I can look forward to the day and time when I will be finished pushing myself to my limits. I can also pace myself and push myself extra hard for the last day or so, knowing that soon I will be able to relax.

If the work project is something that will take several weeks or months to finish, I can go at it again during my next work period or work on another project for variety, then in three of four weeks go back to the long-range project. Since I give myself seven days of free time every fortnight, I can, if I wish, continue to do some work on any long-range or short-range project I like during those days.

My schedule has the added advantage that it is very simple. During every fortnight, every fourteen day period, I will immerse myself for seven days in a row in any work project that I decide beforehand I want to do.

2:15 a.m. Friday March 26.
I am at the Country Style Donuts shop on Wellington Road. My first schedule is working out very well. A person can get an incredible amount of work done if he really works at it with total application for just seven days in a row. I have always wanted to push myself to the limit of my ability for a period of several days in a row. I have never pushed myself to my limits for more than two or three days at a time, at the most. Usually, when I have pushed myself I have done so for only six, eight or twelve hours at a time. I have always been interested in developing my full potential and in helping others to develop theirs. I have also always, since I was a late teenager, been interested in the human-potential movement in all its forms. I have always prized being free of schedules imposed on me by others (i.e. going to school from nine to four or working at a nine-to-five job). Spontaneity has always been important to me. I have always liked to be able to do what I wanted to do on the spur of the moment. I have said to people that I lived an existential life in that I lived by the day without long-term plans and very often with no plans even for the next day.

3:00 a.m. Friday March 26.
I'm at the Country Style Donuts shop. Talked to several of the regular customers I know.

4:30 a.m. Friday March 26.
I am at home on Wellington Road. If at some time in the future I have to work at a nine-to-five job, I could still use my schedule and apply it to the hours when I didn't have to work at the job. My fortnightly schedule will greatly increase my productivity to the point where I will hopefully never have to work at some nine-to-five job where I will be bossed around.

As a rule, those people who have not learned how to organize their time and use it wisely end up taking orders from those who have learned to discipline themselves.

Mother woke me at about eleven a.m. Thursday morning because father wanted some help with the roof of the house as some shingles are off in places. We went up on the roof but the damage was too difficult for us to fix. Father was talking about his tools and the importance of cleaning them up after using them each time so that they would be ready to use when needed. I agreed with what he said. I thought through and meditated on the sensation function in Psychosynthesis. Said hello to our next door neighbour who commented on what a beautiful day it was and also on how beautiful mother's violet and yellow crocuses are by the back door. They are a beautiful blooming touch of Spring. Went over and petted Irish, the neighbour's dog, a really friendly bitch that always likes to be petted. I came in from the garage at twelve noon and meditated for twenty minutes because I couldn't do so earlier.

I made my usual just-for-today promises to myself with regards to not drinking, not losing my temper and not allowing myself to fall into a state of depression. I also decided that I would think of the benefits of doing my intensive journal for seven days, and also of the benefits of working for seven days in a row out of a two week period with complete application. Made my daily affirmation for a good day. I then ate a piece of raisin pie with buttermilk on it and drank some milk while I read a letter Joan wrote to me that I had just got in the mail. I really love that woman. She is so loving, sensitive, and honest. I am very much looking forward to Joan coming here to Western to study this summer. Her programme is going to start on May the twenty-fourth. Joan said she was looking forward to seeing me. She wrote about loneliness stating that, "Now I feel even more the pain of the aged who are so alone." Joan said she read a journal of Fernand Ouellette, a Quebec poet. She wrote, "As a reaction to despair, anguish, he asks if perhaps just to be is an 'affirmation glorieuse.' "

When I talked to Joan on the phone about three weeks ago, I recommended "The Denial of Death," by Becker. Joan is reading Becker and has read the chapter on Kierkegaard, who she'd studied in philosophy at McGill. She expressed how glad she was that I no longer drank.

When I read her letter I thought about how lonely I was and how much I missed her when she left Montreal just after her birthday a year ago last June, to bike to Toronto. She thought she would be back in a couple of weeks but she stayed in Toronto and worked there all summer. I kept expecting her and looking forward to seeing her, but was disappointed. Not too long before that, Lisa, who I'd been seeing, went back home from Montreal to New York City and didn't go back to McGill in the fall.

The two women that I cared for most in Montreal left within weeks of each other, and that got me feeling very lonely and very depressed. As a result — as usual when I got depressed and/or lonely — I drank a lot.

5:30 a.m. Friday March 26.
Wednesday night I talked to Paul Mackenzie about how I used to go out and drink and often get drunk when I was depressed. I said I really have to fight my desire to go out and drink when I get into a very down mood; so I affirm every day that I will not get depressed or drink. I told Paul about the time on September the thirteenth last year when I got drunk, got hit by a car, and freaked out then and also later on at home.

I said that my other just-for-today affirmation is that I won't allow myself to lose my temper. I told Paul how those three things were linked together in my life. When I stopped drinking, I broke a key link of the chain that bound me. I mentioned to Paul that I had been embarrassed in a way to tell people about my daily affirmations although they really help me a great deal. I said that the other day I read in The Toronto Star an article about olympic wrestlers in Canada being taught mental conditioning in order to psyche themselves up for an event. The athletes are taught to do emotional and mental calisthenics. They are taught to use activity words such as "strong, power, confident and aggressive" and to get the imagery of the activity words and their application so that they will be able to make use of them when they need them. I said this kind of mental conditioning was found to have considerable value for the athletes. I told Paul that after I saw that article I was less embarrassed to tell people about my mental conditioning system. Paul said he took a course in hypnosis in Montreal where people were told to imagine clearly in their minds how good they felt, and how happy they were.

6:00 a.m. Friday March 26.
I am at home. Paul said that these imagings of how good one felt really did affect people's emotional well being in a positive way. I told Paul that the practice of T.M. helped me a great deal to stabilize my emotions and keep me on an even keel. Paul talked about the difference in our feelings and reactions to things. He said he couldn't see any point in doing T.M. because he's not anxious, troubled, or under stress. He said he always had a feeling that I was exaggerating when I talked about women and about how much pain and anguish a certain woman caused me. He couldn't empathize with the intensity of many of my emotional reactions to people and situations. When he spoke of imaging in his hypnosis course, I thought about "The Inner World of Daydreaming" by Jerome Singer and recommended the book to Paul. I told him a bit about how good it was.

1:30 p.m. Friday March 26.
I'm at McDonald's on Wellington Road drinking a coffee I got from Brenda. It's incredible how much has happened to me already that I want to record, happened since I got up at noon that is. I'm now engaging in planning time with

regards to today. Another advantage of my fortnightly schedule is that working on a project for seven days in a row concentrates my energies. I have for as long as I can remember scattered my energies on various projects which I tried to do at the same time; consequently, I kept rushing around from one project to the other and got very little accomplished compared to what I could have done if I had concentrated on one thing at one time.

During the next seven days of my fortnightly schedule, I am free to scatter my energies on as many projects as I like. My schedule gives me the best of both worlds. I don't have to abandon my free, spontaneous, existential life style, but only alternate that life style every other week with a highly-disciplined, highly-concentrated and rigorous life style. Since I began my fortnightly schedule Tuesday March twenty-third at ten-twenty p.m., it will be a good idea to begin each fortnightly schedule on the same day of the week and at the same time of the day. Beginnings are very important to me; so that beginning my schedule on the same day and at the same time of day will reaffirm the importance to me of keeping my schedule. It's an ideal, very warm Spring day.

3:25 p.m. Friday March 26.
I am waiting for the Richmond bus on the corner of Wellington and Baseline. I just checked the time with the Bank of Montreal clock. Now I'm on the bus getting impressions of several interesting women who got on the bus at Westminster hospital. One woman, about ninety, looked as if she had one foot in the grave when she got on, but now she is sitting talking to an attractive brown-eyed nurse about twenty-three and speaking in a very alert, animated way, about her grandchildren. She is in good mental condition for her age.

A very beautiful woman in her fifties with big blue eyes and gray hair got on. She looks like a nurse. Her beauty is ageless. Another woman got on, attractive for her age, about sixty-five. She sat and talked to the driver in a very young dynamic manner. She had more life in her than most women half her age. The other woman who got on was a nurse with long brown hair, green eyes, and a very attractive face.

It makes me feel really good to see older people who think and act in a young, aware, vibrant, manner. At the same time it really turns me off to see young people who look, talk, and act like bored, listless, tired, old people. That's how I have looked and acted during periods of my life when I have been in a depressed state. A depressed person acts much like an old person who is tired of life and is just sitting around waiting for death.

4:00 p.m. Friday March 26.
I'm on the Richmond bus at the gates at Western. For at least the past ten years I have had a strong interest in gerontology, the study of the aging process and the aged. It really makes me angry how poorly the aged are treated in this society that worships youth. Most people have all kinds of misconceptions about old people such as the, "You can't teach an old dog new tricks," myth about learning and age. The tragedy is that old people themselves have been conditioned to believe that these myths are true. Society expects old people to act in certain stereotyped ways. If old people refuse to act in such rigid ways, they are said to be, "Not acting their age," and put down.

6:30 p.m. Friday March 26.
I'm on the Richmond bus heading for home. Beautiful colourful sunset. I feel very good, happy, and together.

11:45 p.m. Friday March 26.
I'm at the Latin Quarter drinking tea and enjoying the scene.

10:35 p.m. Saturday March 27.
I'm at the Casino restaurant on Dundas Street drinking coffee. Yesterday was a very good, productive day — a

fully lived day. So much happened that I didn't have time to record most of it in my journal. I got here at about ten-twenty-five. Showed George "The Goof" by Herman Goodden. George told me that Herman was a friend of his. They went through Mountsfield Public School together. I told George that's where I went to school. I said then it was a five room school with two grades in each classroom. George said he lived on Mountsfield Crescent. I asked him if he knew Peggy or her son Jeff. George said he knew them but not very well. He said that Jeff was a few years ahead of him in school. I asked him if he knew a South Collegiate teacher I know who lives on Mountsfield Crescent. George had heard of him but didn't know him.

11:20 p.m. Saturday March 27.
I'm at the Latin Quarter drinking a small coke that I got from Marci. I am now just digging the scene and getting impressions.

12:00 midnight Saturday March 27.
I'm on the Westminster bus at Dundas and Richmond, heading for McDonald's. Saturday was a very good day. I've always found that it takes a tremendous amount of energy to write out an intensive journal while I have been living very fully at the same time. It is very enjoyable to do, yet very exhausting.

12:15 a.m. Sunday March 28.
At McDonald's drinking a coffee I got from Lori, Kathy's sister.

2:00 a.m. Sunday March 28.
I'm at home. I have read a great many self-help books in my time. When the authors talk about the wise use of time, most of them say that, "If you really want to do something you will find the time to do it." At one time I agreed with those authors but I now completely disagree. There are many things in the present that I really want to

do and only a few of them will I find time to do. I agree with what Mary said to me a few weeks ago at McDonald's that creative people, (creative in the broadest sense, i.e. those who have a creative attitude towards life) never have time to do anywhere as much as they would really like to do. Mary said she would need several lifetimes to do all she really wanted to do. I feel the same way.

There are about twenty books I am in the process of reading right now, each of which is important to me. There are several women I want to go out with and really get to know. I want to write more poetry and articles. I have never written a short story, a novel or a play. Every aspect of writing fascinates me and I want to do some writing in every form.

I would also like to try my hand at advertising, writing public service ads, i.e. media ads promoting ecological concerns. The visual arts are becoming more important to me all the time. I want to do many more works of art such as the assemblages in glass preserve jars that I did. I also want to do a series of collages. Right now I want to do a great many things.

I am conscious that I have wasted a lot of time in my life. For several years of my life I was in a rather screwed-up mental state. Now that I am reasonably together, I want to accomplish a great deal. I realize that in a way I am trying to make up for lost time which one can never really do. Lost time is gone forever. Spending valuable time regretting that one has wasted years of one's life is a double loss. In the process of regretting, one ties up one's energies in the past. With the time one spends in regret, one could and should be doing something in the only time anyone ever has — the now — to actualize one's dreams.

It bothers me that I wrote so little in this journal on Saturday. I feel guilty about it in a way; yet the day brought me a lot of good things, very pleasant experiences and valuable insights that I reflected upon but didn't write down. Right now I am thinking about the importance of a 4H club motto, "Learn to do by doing." I have learned a lot by doing this seven day intensive journal.

2:30 a.m. Sunday March 28.
I am at home on Wellington Road. Thursday night, while I was at the opening of the new Smales Pace, I started to get uptight because I thought I might not be able, in seven days, to get down enough journal writing for a book of about a hundred pages. To do that I figured that I needed to write about twenty pages a day on this parchment paper I am now using, in order to get about a hundred pages of print. I thought a lot about this since and I have decided that I want this seven day intensive journal to be published even if the book is only sixty, seventy or eighty pages long. If no one will publish it, I will get it out myself by paying a commercial printer to print it up.

I am doing something that I have never heard of anyone doing before. I have read selections from a large number of journals and I have read a lot about various kinds of journals. I have questioned a great many people about journals. I have asked questions such as: have they ever written a journal or diary? Why did they keep one if they did? Did they let others see it? How much detail did they put in? Did they keep it on a regular basis? etc. I have also asked people if they have read journals or diaries, if so why and which ones did they like best and why. I have asked and continue to ask people these questions because writing journals is my main life work.

I love to read journals, talk about them with others and find out all I can about them. In all my research I have never come across a published journal that was an intensive journal of one week in the life of the author. This is the journal of an ordinary week in my life, the ordinary life of an ordinary person in an ordinary city in an ordinary country.

3:00 a.m. Sunday March 28.
I am at home on Wellington Road. Why, then, should anyone buy this book and read it if it deals with the

ordinary? My answer is that I deeply believe that when one really sees and touches and feels the ordinary things and events in life, they become the extraordinary. Existence itself is The Extraordinary Miracle. These past few days have not been unusual days in my life, yet they have been filled with mystery, beauty, joy and sadness. I am an ordinary person five-feet nine-inches tall, rather thin, with dark brown hair, balding and bearded with green eyes and an average IQ, or so I was told by a guidance teacher and a guidance counsellor. Very ordinary. And yet I regard myself as extraordinary as I so regard everyone else I know.

I am constantly amazed by people who see themselves as very ordinary, who as I get to know them reveal incredible stories of their lives. Many people tell me they have never been anywhere and have lived most of their lives in London which they regard as a "nowhere town." I have lived in London most of my life and haven't travelled widely at all. In fact I've never been off the North American continent. Hell, I've only been in one country besides Canada and that's the U.S. and I haven't spent much time there. I do, however, know the ordinary city of London rather well and the more I get to know the city the more extraordinary it becomes. I love this city very much. It not only is home, it feels like home. Before this begins to sound like a sales pitch for London, let me add that I have lived in, know and love several other Canadian cities, especially Toronto and Montreal which feel like home to me. Although I have never lived in Quebec City I felt at home the first night I was ever there. I loved that city at first sight. Vancouver is another city I love although I have only been there briefly as a tourist.

3:30 a.m. Sunday March 28.
I'm at home. What I am trying to say is that when you know something and love that something, it becomes extraordinary. Canada, an ordinary country, thus becomes for me and a great many others an extraordinary

country. The same people who tell me that nothing interesting ever happens to them, also tell me that nothing very interesting happens in London. They also tell me Canada "isn't where it's at." I ask them what they mean, although I usually know what they are going to tell me. They say that Canada, "isn't where the action is." When I ask them where they believe the action is, they usually say in the U.S. or in Europe.

I say that the action is where you are, wherever you are; only you may have to really look for it. James Russell Conwell wrote a book called "Acres of Diamonds." The book was the text of a speech that he gave thousands of times during many years all over the U.S.A. He talked to people about how they could achieve financial success. His key concept was that the, "acres of diamonds" that many travel far to find, really lies at our feet but — and here is the catch — we really have to dig for the diamonds. I believe that we need to apply this principle, which is thousands of years old and that Conwell applied mainly to financial success, to success in all areas of life. Within this Southwestern Ontario region are opportunities galore to live life to the full.

There are many reasons why I write and publish my writings; the most important is to share my life and loves with others I may never meet or get to know in this lifetime. I also write in order to liberate myself and others from the bonds of oppression. You are living in a state of oppression when you believe that what you do isn't very important.

4:15 a.m. Sunday March 28.
I'm at home. When people believe that what they do doesn't matter very much, they come to believe that they don't matter very much as people. They believe they are powerless to change things in society because they are only one person and, "You can't fight City Hall." With this attitude of course they don't try to change things. They just grumble and complain. Getting people to feel

psychologically powerless is the first and essential step in getting them to feel and act politically powerless. For me, this leads back to the reason why I am writing a journal, an intensive journal of one week in my life, and why I intend to get it published. I see this as a creative act but also as a political act in a broad sense. I am affirming myself as a unique individual who has chosen to record one week of his life, and has chosen to publish that record in order to share himself and his experiences with others.

    I write, lecture, and recite poetry in order to share feelings, knowledge, ideas and insights with others. I see myself as a benefactor of mankind. I don't mean anything grandiose or egotistical by this. I only want to express the fact that I feel a profound sense of gratitude for all that I have received from others that has helped me to enjoy life and to live it as fully as possible. I want to pass on to others what I have been taught by teachers, philosophers, psychologists, writers, artists, etc. Early Saturday morning, before I went to sleep, I thought about how deeply I want to share the mystery and wonder of life, as I experience it, with others. I thought of different modes of expression. I thought that perhaps I could express most fully what I feel in poetry.

4:30 a.m. Sunday March 28.
I'm at home on Wellington Road. I thought of doing a series of impressions for a book. "Impressions" was the title of the series of weekly columns I wrote for The London Free Press when I ceased being a teenager and could no longer call my column "Thoughts of a Teenager." I just recalled a quip that Greg Curnoe made as a group of us were sitting around in the kitchen of his home on Weston Street in London after the annual Nihilist picnic. Greg talked about how we were all getting old and what we would be doing soon. He said, "... and in not too many years, Roy will be writing 'Thoughts of a Senior Citizen' for The London Free Press." I have thought a lot about doing a book which consists of improvisations and

commentaries on the improvisations. William Carlos Williams in "Kora in Hell" used that system. I got the idea from him. There are so many people and places and ideas and feelings I want to write about! I want to do more stream of consciousness writing in poetry and prose because such writing often conveys best what I want to express. My journals have a considerable stream of consciousness element in them which I like. I need to experiment more in all areas of writing.

7:00 a.m. Sunday March 28.
I'm at home on Wellington Road. I thought it was only about five a.m. It's always later than I think. Friday I woke up at noon when Gordon called. Mother called me to tell me he was on the phone. He wants to go to Fanshawe College Tuesday morning at ten a.m. so he can do some photographic portrait studies of me. We are meeting in the cafeteria of the art section which is the cafeteria I most often go to at Fanshawe. After Gordon called I got up and did T.M. for twenty minutes, a very good meditation. I then made my just-for-today promises to myself with regards to not drinking, not losing my temper and not getting into a state of depression. I also promised myself that I would think about the advantages of doing my intensive journal for one week and also that I would think of the advantages of my Fortnightly Schedule. I then made my usual affirmation for a good day. I ran to McDonald's and, as I did, I thought about the feeling function in Psychosynthesis. I got my coffee from Brenda at McDonald's. While I was there, I was thinking about feeling. I thought about the fact that if I could stop drinking after many years of drinking to excess, then so can a great many other alcoholics and problem drinkers. I also thought that, with all the problems I have had over the years with a very strong wild temper, if I can get my temper under control — which I am achieving — then so can others with such strong tempers. Ever since I can remember, I have been prone to bouts of depression. Only

lately have I been successful in fighting off depression. In this also I know that if I can do it so can others.

I am trying in my lifestyle to serve as a good example to others. I am trying as best I can to live my philosophy of life. I and Thou relationships, as Martin Buber describes them in his book "I and Thou", are what is most important in life to me. I am very much and very deeply involved with others. I realize that I can't allow myself to regress, to start drinking again, lose my temper, or get into depressed states, because, if I did, I would then be again on the downward path leading to self-destruction. Not only that, but I would be hurting others, letting down others who had faith in me and who helped me. I would no longer serve as a good example but I would be seen as a pathetic failure. I would pull down others who had believed in the value of the philosophy of life I expressed. I have to wage a heroic fight for myself and for the sake of others.

7:30 a.m. Sunday March 28.

I feel the same way about suicide. I really believe that we have a responsibility to ourselves not to kill ourselves when we are feeling suicidal. We also have a responsibility to others we would deeply hurt in the process. Also we need to realize that if we kill ourselves, our act may act as a catalyst that precipitates other suicides.

I have been very close to killing myself and realize only too well that at such down times a person feels such pain, torment and despair that almost all he can think of is ending his misery. He feels no hope for the future and tends to feel that no one else gives a damn what happens. He feels isolated and alone. Also he often has thoughts of getting revenge, hurting others because they have either hurt him or ignored his sufferings.

"They'll be sorry. They'll all be sorry," we tell ourselves at such times. At such times we tend to feel worthless. We feel that what we do doesn't really matter to anyone and that the world will be better off without us.

I need to, at all times, learn to take responsibility for my actions. I need to realize my oneness with mankind. We are all part of one another and have responsibility to one another. As John Donne put it so well, "No man is an island." I thought of Socrates' words that, "No evil can happen to a good man, either in life or after death." He also said to his captors something to the effect that, "You may kill me but you cannot destroy me." I can only destroy myself, or allow, by my own reaction, another to destroy me.

As I thought about responsibility, I realized that I could never allow myself to regress and that as I lived, I couldn't stand still so that I would have to keep on progressing up the ascending path towards greater awareness and greater self-actualization. I thought a lot about this realization while I was at McDonald's. While I was there a woman came in with her two daughters.

8:00 a.m. Sunday March 28.
I am at home. The woman was attractive but not beautiful. One daughter was about eight. Pretty, with blue eyes and freckles. The other daughter was about seven and one of the most beautiful children I have ever seen in my life. She had alert bright-blue eyes, light-brown hair in braids and a smile that warmed up the whole place. She had a perfect mouth and a small gap between her two front teeth.

When I see a child like that, I really want to have children. When I talked to Paul last Wednesday, I said that I really wanted to have children because I love kids, but I said it would have to be when I am about forty-five because now I am not in a financial situation where I could afford to get married and have children. I told Paul I didn't want to leave it much beyond forty-five because then I might be too old to enjoy them fully. I said my ancestors are long lived so that I will probably live at least into my seventies if I die of natural causes.

If I had a daughter like her, I would tend to be over protective. I would also have a tendency to spoil her. At the same time, I would probably expect too much of her. Someone as beautiful as she is makes people feel good just by her very being. She had a friendly manner and was very perceptive and intelligent. From where I was sitting I could study her without people thinking I was staring at her. She could be an exceptional child model. She had a very expressive face. I was sad to see her leave. I believe I will always remember her face.

10:00 a.m. Sunday March 28.
I'm at home on Wellington Road. I decided I would not go to the Unitarian Fellowship this morning, but keep writing this out because it is going well and I am in the swing of it. When I got to Western Friday afternoon, I gave my seat to a beautiful woman with blue eyes and short curly bright red hair who I had seen before on the bus. Her hair brushed against my face as I went by her, which I liked. I told her that she could have my seat because I was getting off at the next stop anyway. She thanked me. It was just a good excuse to speak to her. I walked through the Pickup cafeteria to see if there was anyone there I knew. There wasn't. I looked through the bookstore and noticed quite a few new books. They have a paperback on "Assertiveness Training" that I want to get. I finally decided to buy "The Conquest of Frustration" by Maxwell Maltz and Raymond Parker. I had never seen the book before and it just came out in paperback.

As I was waiting in line to get in the Elbow Room, I noticed Suzanne ahead of me talking to a friend. I said, "Suzanne how are you?" She held my hand and squeezed it. I gave her a hug and she kissed my cheek which made me feel really good. She is a very warm, affectionate woman. I met her the Friday before with Jerry, Michael, and Bob, three of the people I drank with last November on my last drunk. She had known me for years she said. Suzanne knew me from nineteen-sixty-seven when we were involved in the Student Christian Movement, Vietnam War protest activities and radical politics in general at Western. I didn't recall her from those days. She said we never really talked. She knew Bill quite well and Glen, two activist friends of mine.

In the Elbow Room I ordered a coke which was thirty-five cents and gave the waitress a nickel tip. I had never had her as a waitress before. Said hello to a very pretty, friendly, blue-eyed blonde waitress I know slightly but would like to get to know a lot better. Bought some Saloon Nuts at the food counter for fifteen cents and ate them. Walked through the Elbow Room looking for people I might know. Said hello to Bob and Jerry who were sitting with Suzanne. Picked up a Gazette and read it. Read an article on a friendly acquaintance of mine, Professor Key who taught in the journalism department at Western. Key wrote the book "Subliminal Seduction."

11:00 a.m. Sunday March 28.
I am at home. Friday, I looked through "Oui", "Playboy", and other magazines in the shop across from the Elbow Room. I also checked out the paperbacks. I bought "Penthouse Forum" magazine for the first time because I wanted to read an article in it on depression and also an article on T.M. It cost one dollar. In the Elbow Room I read the first few pages of "The Conquest of Frustration" which I really liked as far as I read.

I left for home Friday at about six-thirty. Around Wellington and Baseline, a woman I hadn't seen in many years got on the bus. She'd been in the same grade as I at Mountsfield school. She has reddish hair and a face covered with freckles. I couldn't recall her name. I thought of going up and telling her I thought I recognized her from public school, but I was afraid to because I thought I might get a negative reaction. I also thought I might have been mistaken, but I doubted very much if I was. I really must work on myself to get rid of such fears, or at least to take action in spite of my fears.

At home I did T.M. for twenty minutes, a good peaceful meditation. I ate some supper, then went up to the Country Style Donuts shop. Marie was my waitress. I looked through The Toronto Star. Bought The London Free Press to see if there were any art openings but there were none.

11:10 p.m. Sunday March 28.
I'm at McDonald's on Wellington Road, drinking a coffee I got from Diana. Said hello to Debbie. Diane is also working. I just said goodbye to Paul Mackenzie who I won't see for another year and a half. I thought about the tremendous amount that has happened to me since I saw Paul and Niti a year ago last October, almost a year and a half ago. It seems like several years ago. Yesterday, and today at Paul's place, I thought about the imaging aspect of Psychosynthesis. Thought about the importance of the ideal model as an image of what one wants to strive for and become. I am working on visualizing myself as being more self-confident and self-controlled and acting in a more confident, self-controlled way. Psycho-cybernetics is helpful to me in this process of visualization.

I thought a lot about the fact that when, in the past, I have acted in a negative way by getting drunk, losing my temper, falling into a state of depression, etc., I have always imagined myself doing those things before I did them. Very often, as in losing my temper, the visualization occurred so quickly before the act of losing my temper, that I wasn't even consciously aware of the process. But the more aware I am of the process, the more I am able to recognize it and control it. When I do my imaging meditation, I try to become as aware as possible of my decision making process and the role played by my imagination.

11:40 p.m. Sunday March 28.
I'm at McDonald's on Wellington Road. I got a second coffee from Debbie. This place was almost full for half an hour with hockey players and fans that came here by bus and car.

4:12 p.m. Monday March 29.

Once again I am at McDonald's, drinking a coffee I got from Joyce. Said hello to Kathy, Lori's sister and to Nancy. Brenda is here and Cindy. I ran home from here at twelve-ten this morning after they closed. I then did T.M. for twenty minutes. A very good, peaceful meditation. I had moments of pure awareness when my mantra disappeared and I was simply very aware. These moments usually only last for a few seconds or at most a minute or two, then thoughts or images once again enter consciousness.

While I meditated, I thought about my love for people. I thought about the fact that I want everything I do to be of benefit to others as well as to myself. I have always wanted to be helpful to people but I have far too often just thought about myself and my own well-being and happiness and not nearly enough about others. This has caused me to be far less considerate in dealing with others than I should have been. I realized that I need to more consciously think about the benefits of my actions on others as well as on myself. I thought of this while I ate dinner and then for a couple of hours in bed before I went to sleep.

This afternoon after I got up, I formulated my concept in this way, "I will endeavour to take every situation that happens to me and turn it to my advantage and to the advantage of others in a mutually beneficial way." I will try to do this in any and every situation that life presents. This attitude towards life involves a creative, problem-solving way of relating to events.

This afternoon while I was washing up, I thought of Socrates' words that, "No evil can happen to a good man either in life or after death." As I thought of those words, one of my favourite phrases to meditate on, I considered the fact that if one acts in a beneficial way in this life, one can still go on benefiting others after one has died, as one's words and memory goes on. Conversely, if one acts in a destructive way towards oneself and others, after one's death one's destructive influence still goes on and continues to hurt people.

This is, of course, an obvious truth and it is something I have thought about many times before. Yet what happens to me and to most people is that we read about, hear about, and think about these obvious truths and say, "Of course that's obvious," and promptly dismiss the thought from our minds.

4:45 p.m. Monday March 29.
I'm at McDonald's on Wellington Road, drinking a coffee I got from Joyce. It is an unfortunate fact that we don't really give deliberate, conscious, thought to obvious truths. If all I accomplish in all my writings and lectures is to get people to stop and consider obvious truths, and to become in the process very aware of these obvious truths, then I will be successful beyond my wildest dreams. This is, after all, what all the prophets and all the teachers of enlightenment have been trying to accomplish throughout history. As Socrates said, "The unexamined life is not worth living." And I think it was Alfred North Whitehead who said that, "The hardest thing to get anyone to undertake is the analysis of the obvious."

It's important to realize that when one acts, one is playing for keeps. There is no second time around, as far as I know. When one is dead, that's it. He has written his own record and the book is closed. I believe in an after-life in the sense that consciousness goes on and one exists on another plane or dimension of being; however, I believe that one is on earth only once — so we had better make the most of it. This is why I am deeply opposed to suicide because, "While there's life there's hope," another obvious truth yet one extremely difficult to see when one is severely depressed and suicidal. Here I am speaking from experience. For several weeks in succession, I thought of suicide every hour of the day and was right on the edge of taking my own life.

During those days, all I did to try to get out of my pain and misery was to get drunk as soon as possible in the day and stay drunk all day. During some of those drunks, I got beaten up, badly injured myself and came close to getting killed in traffic.

5:00 p.m. Monday March 29.

I am at McDonald's. I just didn't give a damn about what happened to me. I didn't see any hope, yet I hung on because of my parents and the friends who loved me and were kind and helpful to me. If I had thought then that things could be as good as they are now for me, then I certainly wouldn't have contemplated suicide. But at that time, I just couldn't see any way out. Part of the reason why I didn't kill myself was that I knew it would cause my friends, parents and relatives a terrible amount of pain and could lead to others killing themselves through a chain reaction. As I write, a cold shiver runs through me as I think of how close I was to ending it all.

For Christ's sake, if you ever get that low, remember that there is hope for you, but also reach out for help to your friends, doctor, minister, whoever you can trust and whoever you find sympathetic and helpful. If you feel suicidal in the middle of the night, call up *Contact*, or your city's twenty-four hour community centre which has a well-trained sympathetic staff of volunteers who are there because they want to help you if you need help, or advice, or just a friendly sympathetic ear to listen to you as you unload your anguish. They will help you by listening, and by giving you advice if you ask for it. If you are in a desperate situation and need more help than they can provide over the phone, they will put you in touch with a community agency or resource person who will provide help. You don't have to be desperate to call them either. It may be three o'clock in the morning and you are really lonely with no one to talk to and need to hear a friendly voice. That's important. But you may be really down and not know the number to call or the name to look up in the phone book. Just call information, that's what I did. They have the number.

5:30 p.m. Monday March 29.
I am at McDonald's. Part of the reason I am writing about this is that I know a lot of people who don't even know that such a service exists in most cities. It's a community organization, a valuable resource that can help anyone at low periods in his or her life. If such a telephone service doesn't exist in your city, then call long distance and ask the operator to give you the number of such a service in the nearest city. If such a service doesn't exist where you live, then why not get together with some friends and start one up! One more thing before I leave this topic — about nine out of ten people who attempt suicide, talk about killing themselves either directly or indirectly. They give some indication of what they contemplate doing. These are calls for help. For God's sake if someone you know is depressed and makes references to killing himself or herself, whether the reference is veiled or not, don't ignore these warning signals but really listen to these people, hear them out, and try to help them, or get them to seek professional help. On the other hand, don't panic. A great many people at one time or another in their lives talk about ending it all. Most of these people will never kill themselves. What I am saying above all is that a person who talks about ending it all, whether the talk is veiled or not, is asking for help either subconsciously or consciously. He or she is saying that he or she is screwed-up, depressed, and needs to be listened to and helped.

6:00 p.m. Monday March 29.
I am at McDonald's on Wellington Road drinking my second coffee that I got from Julie. Whenever any situation occurs that affects me, I will always ask myself the question, "How can I take this situation and turn it to my advantage and to the advantage of others in a mutually beneficial way?"

Ruth Benedict has been an important influence on me with her concept of good societies being those societies with a high degree of synergy and bad societies being low-synergy societies. Before I read her writings on synergy I had heard about synergy from Buckminster Fuller at lectures he had given. His use of synergy greatly influenced me. I had never heard the word before I had read and listened to Fuller. In fact, Fuller did a great deal to popularize the word.

A few years ago I read Ruth Benedict's "Forgotten Manuscript" which was found and introduced by Abraham Maslow who had been a student of hers and greatly influenced by her. Synergy concerns whole systems. The whole of a system is greater than the sum of its parts. Ruth Benedict talked of high-synergy societies as those societies that were structured in such a way that what the individual did to benefit himself benefited the society as a whole. Societies that are structured in such a way that what the individual does to benefit himself does not add to society but rather takes away from and hurts the whole society, are low-synergy societies. A "dog eat dog," highly competitive Capitalist or Communist society is a low-synergy society. A democratic, socialistic society that is concerned with the well-being of its citizens and values the contribution and talents of everyone is a high-synergy society.

6:30 p.m. Monday March 29.
I am at McDonald's on Wellington Road. The kind of mutual aid anarchical society advocated by Peter Kropotkin would be a very high-synergy society. This mutual aid is altruism in action. In such a society one does not need to unselfishly sacrifice oneself for the good of the State, or the Cause, or the approved religion. On the other hand, in a society with high-synergy, selfishness is seen as very stupid and shortsighted. If people live in a society where they are free to grab as much as they like in terms of money or property or power, then they are never secure with what they have grabbed because they know that others will try to grab from them what they have. Such individuals operate according to the zero sum economic

model. Life is seen as involving a series of transactions where, if I win you lose, if you win I lose.

A great deal of this way of thinking has pervaded the thinking of War Games theorists such as Herman Kahn who deal with win and lose strategies involving thermonuclear war and megadeaths. This zero sum theory and world view dominated the economic theory of Malthus and the social and economic theory of the Social Darwinists. This thinking can also be seen exhibited by the "Lifeboat Ethics" advocates. These people see the world as having a scarcity of natural resources. There is, according to these people, not enough for everyone so they intend to get theirs while the getting is good, then defend themselves and what they have against the have-nots who would take it from them. People like Buckminster Fuller believe that there will be enough food and resources for all, once people begin to see that it is in the self interest of people and nations to share the benefits of technology with the have-nots. Fuller very realistically and synergistically speaks of the earth as Spaceship Earth. Nations as well as individuals need to live with a high degree of synergy in a true parliament of mankind. Because I believe this, I support the extremely important work being done by the World Federalists all over the world to create a true world government.

8:00 p.m. Monday March 29.

I'm at home. Hans Selye, world expert on stress who has done a great deal of research in the field at the University of Montreal, in his recent excellent book "Stress Without Distress" says that one should, "Earn thy neighbour's love." This is the kernel of his philosophy of life. He believes we should be useful to others. In that way we get love, respect, and gratitude from others. He calls such behaviour "altruistic egoism." Selye believes that such behaviour will make us happy and beneficial human beings. He also believes that such behaviour will provide us with security from the aggression of others because, who wants to harm someone who is useful and beneficial?

I thought of how this ties in with Transcendental Meditation with its emphasis not only on individual well-being and fulfillment but also on the harmony, orderliness and well-being of society. As I thought of that, I just thought of the book "T.M. Discovering Inner Energy and Overcoming Stress" by Bloomfield, Cain, Jaffe and Kory and I recalled that Hans Selye wrote the foreward to the book and Buckminster Fuller wrote the introduction. I just reread the introduction and foreward. I am very much in agreement with these three teachers of mine — Buckminster Fuller, Hans Selye, and Maharishi Mahesh Yogi. I call them my teachers because over the years I have been profoundly influenced by their lives and thoughts. I read "The Stress of Life" and articles on the book not too long after it came out in fifty-six. Around that time I read an excellent article by Selye in "Maclean's" magazine. In the article I was impressed by Selye's earlier version of his philosophy of life. Since then I have read many other articles on him and by him. Don Bell just recently told me about the interview of Selye he did for "Air Canada." Don was very impressed by Selye as a person.

9:15 p.m. Monday March 29.

At home. I heard Maharishi Mahesh Yogi speak about ten years ago in the Middlesex College auditorium at the University of Western Ontario. Paul Mackenzie mentioned to me the other night that he went with me at that time to hear Maharishi speak. Paul thought Doug might have gone with us but he wasn't sure. I thought perhaps Les went with us too. About two or three years before that, I had been initiated along with Peter, John, and Anita by one of Maharishi's initiators in a room at the Belvedere Hotel in London, Ontario. Two days before we were initiated, we went to hear Maharaj speak at a hall on King Street. John saw the announcement in The London Free Press about the free lecture and knowing my interest in meditation and mysticism, he called me up to tell me about it. We went to hear Maharaj and liked what he had to say. We wanted to check him out, so we got together the next day with him in his room at the Belvedere. We asked Charlie Savage to come along. So there we were — Anita, Charlie, John, Peter, and myself. Charlie was, to say the least, sceptical. We were all very impressed by the way Maharaj, the Indian guru, handled Charlie's cross-examination and critical attack. Charlie was in India during the second-world-war and he held a not too high opinion of Indian "Holy Men." Maharishi came to Toronto to lecture at the height of the Hippie Flower Power movement. I remember at the time rushing around Yorkville telling people that they should go and hear him. I also got some ads for the lecture and put them up in boutiques and restaurants in Yorkville.

9:45 p.m. Monday March 29.
I told everyone I knew, and anyone who would listen to me, about the lecture, including two very good friends, Don and Carolyn, who didn't go to hear Maharishi because they thought it was all a lot of nonsense. Since then, Don has been initiated and practices T.M. I believe Carolyn does also, but I'm not sure. The day after the talk, the meditators were invited back to hear Maharishi speak, and meditate with him in a group (that was my first group meditation), and ask him questions about the meditation. I was deeply impressed with Maharishi then and I continue to be deeply impressed with him and the T.M. movement.

Buckminster Fuller I first heard at Convocation Hall, at the University of Toronto, and also the next day at the U. of T. school of Architecture. Two years later, I heard him speak a couple of times at the University of Western Ontario. Later I got to meet him and talk to him after a lecture he gave at the Holiday Inn on King Street. It was a by invitation only event. The invitations went to selected members of the community. Needless to say I was not invited. Quite a few people were uptight when I showed up and wondered how I had gotten into the event. The president of the students' council, John Yokom of Western University, a friend of mine, had an invitation but couldn't go and he knew I really wanted to attend; so he had me go as his alternate with his invitation.

Fuller is without a doubt one of the most incredible speakers I have ever heard. He is a man, now in his late seventies, who can hold an audience spellbound for two to three hours or more without a note and with a rapid delivery. In that time he covers an incredible amount of ground taking you on a "Fuller trip." If you ever get a chance to hear Fuller, don't pass up the opportunity. If you want to get into Fuller and haven't read anything by him I recommend "I Seem To Be A Verb", "Utopia or Oblivion", or "An Operating Manual For Spaceship Earth." These books are easier and less technical than others he has written.

10:00 p.m. Monday March 29.

Early this morning, before I went to sleep, I thought a lot about how to best communicate my thoughts and feelings through the written word. I want to write many more portraits of people and places I love. Rilke writes that the poet's mission is "to praise and to cherish." There are so many people and things I want to praise and to cherish!

11:02 p.m. Monday March 29.

Once again it is later than I thought it was. I thought it was only ten-thirty. When I think about it, I check Dan Brock's historical calendar of London put out by Applegarth, to see what happened ten, twenty, fifty, or more years ago in London. I see that on March twenty-ninth, eighteen-forty-five, "Royal assent was given to the provincial bill reincorporating the defunct Great Western Rail Road Company (formerly the London and Gore Rail Road Company)." That kind of information intrigues me because I am deeply into history and nostalgia.

What I want to say about people and their lives was said in an incredibly beautiful way by Yevgeny Yevtushenko in his poem "People." He talks about his poetry being a lament he makes against destruction. He believes as I do that no people are uninteresting. He speaks about the fact that when people die, worlds die in them. He finds interest even in people who have lived their lives in obscurity. I heard Yevtushenko read his poems in Russian and English at McGill two years ago. Afterwards at the reception I met him, told him I was a writer and that his poem "People" expressed beautifully and perfectly what I felt about people and had never been able to express anywhere near as well. He thanked me and recited for me a few lines from "People" and from "Colours" which I told him expressed the way I feel about a woman I love. He asked me if I wrote poetry and when I said I did he asked me to recite a poem but I declined the invitation.

On that occasion I saw Sheila, a good friend of Charlie Savage's. She was with Laurence Hutchman, a Montreal poet and good friend of mine, from years ago when he went to Western. Laurence also knew Charlie. Sheila asked me if I had seen Charlie lately because she knew I lived in London. I told her that he had died a week or two before that. I said I was in Montreal at the time but that my mother wrote to me saying that Ed had called me from Forest to tell me about Charlie's death. I showed them the obituary notice that mother sent. This really stunned Sheila because Charlie had called her less than a month before that and sounded in good spirits at the time. Sheila asked me how Charlie had died but I didn't know.

Charlie lived an obscure life as far as the world went. He spent most of his working life as a janitor. For years he was verger of St. Paul's Cathedral in London, Ontario; yet he lived an incredible life, touching many people — and when he died, worlds certainly died in him. How to praise and cherish such people? Mentioning them in my journals is one way. Writing poems about them is another way. I intend to do more poetic sketches of people and places. I want to get down really clear images. All of this writing is to a great extent stream of consciousness, yet why shouldn't it be? I am writing about what I am thinking, feeling, and perceiving from moment to moment.

Don Bell called me from Montreal last Tuesday morning and as he talked to me about "Pocketman", the book he wrote on me, he described his stream of consciousness sections on the contents of my pockets as "stream of nothingness" writing, a quip which I really enjoyed. My journal style has been influenced by Freud and psychoanalysis with its free association and also by the Surrealists such as André Breton and Lawrence Ferlinghetti whose book "Her" is one of my favourites.

11:45 p.m. Monday March 29.
James Joyce also has had a strong influence on me. I finally got to sleep at about four a.m. today and slept till three p.m. I had meditated for about fifteen minutes when Dave called. He sounded a lot better. I told him that Paul Mackenzie, whom I had mentioned to him a number of times before, was in London for most of the week. Told Dave I would drop over to see him on Wednesday. I also mentioned the photography exhibit, "Southern Exposure", at the McIntosh Gallery — done by Fanshawe students. Told Dave I was going to Fanshawe tomorrow to get my picture taken by one of the students. I said I was getting a free print. He asked me to get another one for him and he would pay me for it so he could put it on the mantle in his living-room. I said I considered it an honour that he would want a picture and that I would be glad to give him one. I told him that I was doing a great deal of writing these days. We spoke about the importance of living life with intensity.

After the call I again meditated for fifteen minutes. Made my just-for-today promises to myself about not drinking, not allowing myself to lose my temper, and not falling into a state of depression. I thought of the wording for my just-for-today affirmation to myself, with regards to benefiting myself and others in all that I do. My formulation of this affirmation will be that, "Just for today

I will endeavour to take every situation that happens to me and turn it to my advantage and the advantage of others in a mutually beneficial way." This is an affirmation that I will repeat to myself every day after I do T.M. to condition my mind for the day. Now I have four just-for-today promises I make to myself once every day along with any other affirmations I might want to make use of for one or two or a few days at a time. I then made my affirmation for a good day. As I dressed and washed, I thought about Socrates' words on death and goodness, evil and destruction.

12:15 a.m. Tuesday March 30.
At McDonald's. I ran here and as I ran I thought about the impulse and desire aspects of Psychosynthesis. I was going to go to the Latin Quarter at ten p.m. but my writing was going along so well that I decided not to go. Then at eleven, I thought of going to McDonald's but decided against it. I just finished eating a very leisurely dinner before I left home. Right now I am catching up on my journal and recording more of the events of Friday that I didn't have time to record before.

At around nine p.m. Friday, I chatted with Marie for a while at the donut shop. She was reading "Lives of Girls and Women" by Alice Munro, but found it boring. She heard they had banned it from school libraries. I finished reading the article on depression in "Penthouse Forum." It was a good sound article but I learned very little about the subject that I didn't know before. I started talking to Gary who was in anthropology at Western. He said he dropped out of school because he didn't have enough money to pay his rent. He asked me how my writing was coming along. I told him it was coming along very well. He said he hadn't seen me around. I used to run into him a lot at three or four o'clock in the morning at the donut shop. I showed him "The Goof" by Herman Goodden. I mentioned that Herman was only twenty-two and that "The Goof" was his first published book.

He read a few pages then asked where he could get a copy. I told him where he could get Applegarth publications. I showed him Dan Brock's "Historical Calendar of London" and his almanacs. He took a look through "The Ledger" by Robert Kroetsch, "Rhythms" by Les Arnold, and "Ten Letters" by Colleen Thibaudeau. I asked him if he had heard of James Reaney at Western but he hadn't.

12:45 a.m. Tuesday March 30.
I am at home on Wellington Road. Gary and I got into a discussion of regionalism. I told him that I was very much involved with regionalism in that I am deeply concerned with my roots and the roots of my parents and grandparents who have lived their lives in Southwestern Ontario. Both my parents were born within seventy-five miles of London as were my grandparents. I said I believed that it was very important that people get to know their region, its history and its culture. I said that there is a growing interest among people in this area in regionalism and that Applegarth, a London Ontario publishing company, is making a valuable contribution to this developing interest.

I told Gary that I knew Herman, that I met him through Winston last November when the London Public Library sponsored a reading of Applegarth authors in the auditorium of the library. When I heard Herman read, I was impressed with the strength and vividness of his imagery and I liked his use of dialogue. Afterwards I told him how much I enjoyed his reading. It wasn't until sometime later at an art show in the art gallery at the main library that I really got to talk to him. He talked about his days at South Collegiate and I talked about my days there. A week ago I read Ross Woodman's review of Herman's book. I then read "The Goof" up to page thirty. I haven't read any more of it since, not because I didn't enjoy it but because I did enjoy it. When I read a book I really enjoy I often read it a few pages at a time, think about it, then read some more. I like Herman and I like his writing and he is writing about the Forest City that I love, so I intend to read the book very slowly.

I don't know how good a book it is and I will probably never know because when someone I know and like writes about a person or persons or a place I really like, I have a strong bias in favour of the book, article, play, or poem. However, I do try to be reasonably objective in all my reading.

1:30 a.m. Tuesday March 30.
I am at home. If a friend of mine anywhere has written something about anything at all, I want to read it and I will buy it if I can possibly afford it. While I am at it, I might just as well confess that when I buy a book from an author I know, or buy it in a bookstore, I like to have it autographed. It's more personal that way. Since this is confession time, I might as well mention that I collect autographs or rather that I used to several years ago. I no longer have the habit. My most prized autograph is that of Louis Armstrong, that I got from Louis after a concert he gave here in London at the Gardens about ten years ago. I love jazz and he was my favourite jazz singer and musician.

I told Gary at the donut shop that I was writing a journal about my day-to-day life in London. I told him I had written journals for twenty-five years and that I had written them with regularity for twenty years.

2:00 a.m. Tuesday March 30.
I am at home on Wellington Road. Friday at the donut shop, I chatted a bit with Marie, and with several of the regulars, then paid Lulu for my coke and left. Went to the Red Lion pub. Pete was there. He was glad to see me, shook my hand and invited me to sit down for a beer. I told him I stopped drinking four months ago. Said hello to John who wants me to get him a copy of "The Goof." John got me a ginger ale with his compliments. Said hello to Jeremy and asked

him if he got me the colour prints I wanted of the pictures he took of me at the Home County Folk Festival at Victoria Park in London. He didn't get them made up yet. Said he keeps forgetting.

I sat at the table with Pete. He is really going through hard times. Pete is staying at the Salvation Army Hostel and is out of work. He was really raging about Trudeau and his wage and price controls. He said it's always the guy on the bottom that gets screwed. I agreed with him on that one-hundred percent. We talked of good times years ago at the Lion with Ken, John and the rest of the crowd. Pete said he has a four-year-old niece out West that he has never seen and never held in his arms. He said, "You know how much I love kids Roy. I just want to hold my little niece in my arms before I die." Then he started to cry and said he might not live much longer. For all his hard times, he looked reasonably healthy. Although he was rather shabbily dressed, I have been worse dressed at times. I gave him an ad for Winston's book, "Parts of People in These Parts", and told him that Ken and I were in the book. Pete spoke of how fond he was of Ken and I. Pete said some people put us down but he always stands up for us because we are good people.

2:30 a.m. Tuesday March 30.

I'm at home. Pete is a sad person in some ways, yet has a certain nobility. He is basically a decent, good-hearted person and I enjoy talking to him. Kevin came by and said, "Where the hell have you been Roy?" I told him I hadn't been in the pub much in the past few months because I had stopped drinking four months ago. He said, "Good for you Roy." I asked him how Don and Frank were doing. He said, "Oh they're around." I shook hands and wished him well. When I left the Lion I ran down Dundas Street and up Richmond Street to the Latin Quarter.

Walked all through the Latin Quarter as I usually do to see if anyone that I knew was there. Winston called me over. He and his friends were sitting with a couple of guys

I was introduced to but whose names I forgot. Winston shook hands. I took Judy's hand and kissed it. It was really good seeing Winston and his friends because I hadn't seen them for some time. I told him I was sorry that he couldn't come over the other night to meet Paul. Winston didn't think he had ever met Paul and I wasn't sure if he had or not. I asked Winston when he was going to have me at his high school to talk to his class about Malcolm Lowry. I spoke a year ago last October to some of his classes. They were taking Canadian short stories and one of the stories they took was actually a section from "Under the Volcano", one of my favourite books. "Under the Volcano" is the best book ever written on an alcoholic by an alcoholic. It's appropriate that I lost my annotated copy on a drunk a few years ago.

3:30 a.m. Tuesday March 30.
At home. I really enjoyed lecturing at Winston's school but then again I have enjoyed lecturing or really talking to students in Barry's class at Lucas, John's class at Oakridge, a Man and Society class at Central and at public schools, high schools, community colleges and universities in London, Toronto, and Montreal. I really got off on talking with students in the art classes of Maurice, Chris, and Ken at Sir George Williams University in Montreal. The youngest kids I have ever lectured to were about nine years old and were students in Bill's class at a public school in Toronto. I've also lectured in high school classes in Toronto. I could write a book just on my experiences lecturing to school groups, Liberal Religious Youth groups, Unitarian fellowships, and many other church and discussion groups. I have also taken many topics and spoken on them in groups ranging from the Club Eight-thirty at Metropolitan United Church to the Forum, a Sunday afternoon discussion group I started up around fifteen years ago. I showed Winston and his friends "Transcanada Letters" by Roy Kiyooka. I told them that Roy is an art teacher, painter, photographer and poet. I

said I got the book at the Forest City Gallery at Ron Martin's opening. I said I asked Greg Curnoe if it was for sale and he said it was. He said he hadn't seen it before because if he had he would have gotten it himself. Goldie said they had one more which I believe he did get.

4:00 a.m. Tuesday March 30.
I am at home on Wellington Road. I told Winston and his friends that what Roy Kiyooka was trying to do with his book of letters (at least what I think he was trying to do), I am trying to do with my journals. I mentioned that I never met Roy when he was an art teacher at Sir George Williams but that I had lectured in classes taught by friends of his such as Chris and Maurice. Also he taught many friends of mine who spoke well of him. I said Roy wrote letters to people I know such as George and Angie Bowering. As I went to show them a passage, they said to sit down so Judy moved over and I sat on half of her chair and said, "Hey I really like this. It's cosy." So saying I gave her a hug.

I showed them parts of a letter where Kiyooka commented on Michael Ondaatje's article in "20 Cents Magazine" on his show in London, Ontario. Kiyooka called it "20 Cents Review." That little magazine did a lot to stimulate regionalism. I always enjoyed reading the magazine partly because most of the people who wrote for it were friends of mine. I eagerly awaited each issue to find out what Ron Martin was going to say on Ronnie's Page, or Murray Favro in Murray Favro's Journal or Hugh McIntyre in Uncle Hugh Sez or Greg Curnoe in Greg Curnoe's Radio Journal. I also enjoyed writing for the magazine. I wrote poetry, articles, essays, and a series on my experiences at the Woodstock Pop Festival. Once Maureen, my girlfriend at the time, and I made the cover of the magazine, which is the first time and last time I have ever been on the cover of any magazine.

Bob McKenzie, the editor, was a very good, conscientious editor who I found pleasant to work with.

The magazine stopped publishing a few years ago. It is to Bob's credit that while it lasted, it was a very good, informative magazine that provided an important forum — the only magazine forum, in fact, for local writers.

4:30 a.m. Tuesday March 30.

Years before "20 Cents Magazine" began to publish, Greg Curnoe published "Region" which was, as the title implies, a regional magazine. It was much less ambitious an undertaking than 20 Cents and came out only irregularly, yet at the time it was the only local magazine for regional writers and was significant because of that. Greg wanted me to write something for the magazine but when I finally got around to writing something, "20 Cents Magazine" was coming out again under new management. It had been out before as a slimmer less widely circulated magazine. Around that time, Greg stopped publishing "Region" and my piece, "The Answer Questioned", appeared in "20 Cents Magazine." After I showed Winston and his friends "Transcanada Letters", I reached in my bag, pulled out the Applegarth books and calendar, spread them around the table and came on like a salesman selling his wares in a high-pressure way. They all got a chuckle out of that. I said, "Talk about 'Death of a Salesman'!" I told them after I went to see "Death of a Salesman" at Theatre London, I talked to a couple of people, friends of mine, as we were waiting to get into the Latin Quarter afterwards. I told them how I identified with some of the people in the play and how the family scene in the play resembled mine in a way. I said to them that I used to be a salesman. Just after that Joel saw me and asked me if I was still selling the London historical calendars. I said I was, got one out of my club bag and sold it to him. Then I said to my friends, "Used to be a salesman! Hell, I still am a salesman!" Winston said he and some friends were thinking of renting the downstairs party room at the Latin Quarter for his record launching party.

5:00 a.m. Tuesday March 30.
After Winston and his friends left I sat over on a couch. I was served by a pretty, slim woman with short black hair and delicate features. I had a cup of tea which cost fifty cents. It was my first cup of tea at the Latin Quarter. Said hello to Maurice who was singing. As I left I spoke to Vi, a very friendly warm waitress who I really like. Lynn, the hostess, was wearing a long black dress. Although she looks good in anything, she looked especially good in that dress. As I left I put my arm around her and gave her a hug. She is a very beautiful woman, beautiful in every way. She always makes me feel good. I said hello to other waitresses I knew. As I sat there drinking my tea, I thought of how much the Latin Quarter, its people and atmosphere, means to me and has meant to me over the years. I could write a book about the place. I have in my journals several pages of conversation I had with Sue when I first dated her there. I have written a great deal in my journals now that I come to think about it, about my times there, my dates there with various women and my thoughts and feelings while I was there alone or with a woman. I once bought a glass of Canadian wine for Andrei Voznesensky when he went there after reciting poetry at Western. At that time he invited me to his table but I declined the offer because he was with a group from Western and I didn't want to intrude. When I declined, he asked me to join him and some friends the next morning in his room at the Hotel London. That invitation I accepted. I proceeded on that occasion to get drunk rapidly as we tossed back straight vodka and toasted each other. I had never before had the experience of tossing back liquor.

5:30 a.m. Tuesday March 30.
I am at home on Wellington Road. I told Mrs. Downs about Voznesensky being at the Latin Quarter, so she went over and got him to sign the guest book. The memories associated with the Latin Quarter are really starting to flood into my consciousness but I have to get on with this journal.

6:00 a.m. Tuesday March 30.

I am at home on Wellington Road. I am very conscious of the fact that I haven't recorded my dreams in this intensive journal. Some of them I should have recorded but most of them were very jumbled up and didn't make sense. Just the same, there were some dreams I could have profitably recorded but they were very few and I believe of little significance. I am also aware that I haven't been recording what I ate and how I liked what I ate except at the beginning of this intensive journal. Although I really enjoy eating, I don't regard the description of what I ate or the taste and smell of what I ate to be as important as other things I want to record; so those are the things I left out. It's all a matter of priorities. On Saturday I was exhausted. I thought a lot and so didn't get to sleep till about three or four a.m. Saturday. I slept till around four p.m. when Mary called to tell me she couldn't see me on the weekend. She was feeling depressed. We talked for a few minutes. I went back to sleep, woke up and thought and then slept till about nine p.m. I then got up and did T.M. for twenty minutes. Made my just-for-today promises to myself with regards to not drinking, not losing my temper, and not falling into a state of depression. Then I made an affirmation for a good day.

I was at the Casino at ten-thirty on Saturday night. I said hello to the very pretty blue-eyed blonde with freckles who works there. She said, "Hello how are you?" I said, "Really good." As I left I asked George Mahas if he minded if I mentioned him by name in my journal. I told him that I wrote down whatever happened to me of interest during the day and that I would probably write down that he was an old friend of Herman Goodden's and that he went through Mountsfield school with him. I said to George that he and I often had discussions that I found interesting and sometimes recorded. He said he didn't mind if I used his name. I paid thirty cents for the coffee I had and ran to the Latin Quarter. Barb was working on cash. The pretty woman who served me Friday night was working. Also a new girl I met on St. Patrick's Day. A very sexy woman. I asked Barb if she had heard of "The Goof" by Goodden. She hadn't. I was going to show her a copy but I decided to wait till another time. I sat on the couch where I sat the night before. Marilyn, the friendly woman who goes to Western, was working. I said hello to her and asked her how school was going. She said school was almost over which was a relief. Cheryl and a girlfriend of hers sat right behind me at a table for two. We got talking. I showed her a copy of "The Goof," She said she would like to get it but didn't have the money then. I told her to take it and pay me when she could because I always see her around. This she did. She told me that Ross Woodman teaches her Canadian literature this year. She asked me how my writing was going. I told her it was going well. I really got off on the whole scene. I paid Marci for the coke I drank. I gave her seventy-five cents and told her to keep the change. I didn't realize they have small cokes, ginger ales, etc. and big ones with a cherry and a piece of orange. The tall ones are seventy-eight cents and the small ones fifty-three cents. I told Marci I was going to Fanshawe Tuesday morning to be photographed by Gordon. I told Marci I was going to meet him in the arts cafeteria. She said she often goes to that cafeteria so she might see me there. I like Marci very much. She is a real sweetheart.

7:00 a.m. Tuesday March 30.
I am at home on Wellington Road. I shook hands and said goodbye to Cheryl. I really want to get to know her better. She is an extremely intense person. Her deep brown eyes convey a lot of feeling. I first got to know her when she worked at the Country Style Donuts shop on Wellington Road. Left for the bus. On the way I ran into Gary Wallace the folksinger. I showed him "The Goof" by Goodden. I told him about the author and about the fact that he was writing about London. Gary said he would like to get the book but couldn't afford it at the time. I told him to take it and pay me any time he had the money. I said I

trusted him so there was no problem. He said that by a really strange coincidence he wrote a song called "The Goof." Gary is only twenty-two or twenty-three and already he has written two songs that I consider to be excellent. I believe he will go a long way as a song writer and performer. He is also sincere and friendly which is a considerable asset.

I told the usual friendly bus driver that I thought I would go to McDonald's, so he let me off right in front. I told him that my name was McDonald and that I live on Wellington Road a few blocks from McDonald's. I said that when friends of mine who are parents introduce me to their little children as Roy McDonald, the kids start to call me Ronald McDonald and think McDonald's is my place. He got a kick out of that. He asked me how I liked their hamburgers and I told him that I was a vegetarian.

After I got my coffee I sat down in a section away from my favourite section near the fireplace, because other people were sitting there. When they left I started to move over there but a beautiful woman near me smiled at me.

7:30 a.m. Tuesday March 30.
I'm at home. I smiled back at the woman who I couldn't recall; then she said hello and I said hello. I looked at her in puzzlement. She said, "You don't know me but you know a friend of mine. You met her last week at an art opening." I went over to talk to her and introduced myself. Her name was Elizabeth. She had beautiful clear blue eyes, a well shaped face and reasonably long silky dark brown hair. She invited me to sit down which I did. Lynn, her friend, whom I had met, takes graphics with her at Fanshawe College. Elizabeth said that the next day after Lynn met me she told her about me. Lynn said I had a beard, wore a white trench coat and wrote on a clipboard and that I really observed people carefully. From that description Elizabeth knew I had to be the person Lynn described. That really made my day. Elizabeth does a lot of photography and she

develops her own pictures. I told her that I was going out Tuesday to be photographed at Fanshawe. I told her I really liked Lynn. She said, "Yes she's really nice." I mentioned that I had called Lynn but she wasn't in. I met Rob, Elizabeth's boyfriend who is with the London Flying Club. He has flown for the past three or four years. I mentioned to them that I had learned the trade of instrument technician in the Royal Canadian Air Force but that I had never flown in a plane then or since. She said her father was in the navy but hadn't been aboard ship. She said he gets sea-sick easily. I said I'm uptight about flying in planes. They asked me what kind of writing I did and I told them. I told them about my journals and about how long I had kept them. I got a second coffee and went back to sit with them. I introduced Elizabeth and Rob to Ken, one of the managers, and told him about how Elizabeth recognized me.

7:40 a.m. Tuesday March 30.
I'm at home. Ken said, "You don't see too many people with long beards walking around with clipboards writing notes." I liked Elizabeth a lot and Rob seemed friendly. I told Elizabeth I found it easy to remember her name because I was engaged to a woman named Elizabeth. I showed them the Applegarth publications I had with me. She liked them from the graphics point of view. They didn't have the time to read anything. I also showed Ken the publications. One of the students cleaning up saw the London historical calendar and wants to get one. Ken got me another coffee which I took home to drink to keep me up and at my journal. I wrote this journal till noon on Sunday. Then I lay down and slept till about six-thirty when I called Paul to wish him and Niti bon voyage. He wasn't in when I called. Bruna answered. She and John had just seen "One Flew Over The Cuckoo's Nest." I told her I had seen the movie, so we discussed it. Then Paul came in and I talked to him. I told him to save the pieces he still has of my art work assemblage. The preserve jar the assemblage was

in got broken as their luggage got badly shaken up in flight to Indonesia but Paul said he managed to retrieve some of the assemblage pieces which were scattered all through the rest of the luggage. I said if he could give me the pieces I would take them and add others to them to make up a new one. He said he would do this. I said I would write and he said if I wrote he would write back. I told him to save all my letters. He saved the letter I wrote to him and Niti last summer from the Home County Folk Festival. Paul gave me his address. I asked Paul if I could use his name and what I remembered of our conversations during the week (except what was said in confidence of course), and include the material in my journal for publication. He said I could and that he didn't mind at all.

7:50 a.m. Tuesday March 30.
I am at home. I was going to say goodbye and wish Paul and Niti bon voyage. However, Paul unexpectedly invited me over to his place to look at some slides he took in Java and Bali that he was going to show to his friends John and Bruna who were renting his house. He said he would come around for me at seven-thirty. I did T.M. for twenty minutes. Then I made my usual just-for-today promises to myself. Following that I made my regular affirmation for a good day. Paul talked to my parents for a few minutes in the living room; then I took him downstairs to look at my books on the shelves of mother's fruit cupboard that she had not used for years and I had converted to book shelves. I showed Paul our soft water cistern and asked him if he had ever seen one before. He hadn't. I showed him our dumb-waiter and lathe. I said my father used the lathe from time to time. Paul then looked through some of the books I recommended.

9:27 a.m. Tuesday March 30.
I'm on the Oxford East bus heading for Fanshawe College to get my picture taken. At eight a.m. I did T.M. for twenty

minutes. Gordon called at eight-thirty as I had asked him to, to check to see that I got up in time to see him at ten and to verify arrangements. I made my usual just-for-today promises to myself about not drinking, not losing my temper, and not falling into a state of depression and that just for today, with regards to every situation that happens to me, I will ask myself how I can take the situation and turn it to my advantage and the advantage of others in a mutually beneficial way. Then I made my affirmation for a good day. I showed mother a picture that Gordon took in Mexico of a mother and child. She really liked the picture. I also told mother about how I met Elizabeth at McDonald's the other night, how she knew me from Lynn's description of me. I got on the Richmond bus at Rowntree Park. The driver said, "How are you this morning?" I said, "Fine thank you how are you?" Then he said, "How's your Dad?" He used to work with father at Richard Wilcox a few years ago. He said that he and several others had lots of fun goofing off work for a while and chatted and smoked in the boiler room where my father worked as a stationary engineer. I introduced myself to the bus driver, Chas, who said he had seen me around for years and knew who I was. Chas said he was a friend of George's and was there at George's several times when father was there. He said that Mr. Robinson, owner of Robinson's Industrial Crafts, got his start using my father's wood lathe. He said he once helped father wheel the lathe back to our place in a wheelbarrow. He asked how father was. I told Chas to drop over some time. I asked Chas how he liked his job. He said he likes driving the bus because he gets to meet a lot of really nice people. I told him about Winston's book "Parts of People In These Parts." Chas knows George Goth, Benny Eckardt and others in the book. He even knew Charlie Savage to see. He said, "Didn't he die a little while ago?" I told him that Charlie was one of my best friends. We talked a bit about Charlie. I got off at York Street to go to Applegarth where I bought some copies of "The Goof" and got a photocopy of

Ross Woodman's article in the London Free Press on the book. I told Mac I liked the review.

10:00 a.m. Tuesday March 30.
I am at Fanshawe College. I haven't been at Fanshawe since last November. Michael said that Applegarth would be glad to list colour photostats of my framed journal sketches in their catalogue of works done by local artists and writers for sale. People send in their orders to Applegarth who process the orders and charge the artist or writer a certain percentage of the sales price as commission. Michael said he believed that the colour photostats would sell as well or better than the originals because of the striking colours obtained in the photo-copy process. He said that way I would still have my original and it would become more valuable in the process. He said I wouldn't need to get the photostats made up to sell till the orders came in. He mentioned this very briefly to me at the opening of Ron Martin's show at the Forest City Gallery. The idea appeals to me very much. I said I would be happy for them to list my journal sketches. I want to do a series of collages which I have planned to do for some time and make photo-copies of them with the new Xerox colour-copier to sell.

Mac told me I was still welcome to use a table in their printing studio to work at editing my journals. I told Mac that I had been doing some writing that I thought he might enjoy but I didn't describe what I was doing. I said I would show him and Jill what I had been doing in a couple of days. He said he would be looking forward to seeing it. As I left he mentioned the Wittgenstein conference Western University is holding on the weekend at the Holiday Inn downtown. He had mentioned the conference to me in February but I had forgotten when it was. I have always been interested in Wittgenstein ever since I first read him and read about him and his philosophy about fifteen years ago.

7:35 p.m. Tuesday March 30.
I'm at home on Wellington Road. Mary called me at four-thirty and again at seven-twenty-five. She is going to be able to see me at eight-thirty at McDonald's.

8:05 p.m. Tuesday March 30.
I'm now at McDonald's. I said hello to Diane and Karen who were sitting here with some customers. I guess they just got off work. There is one section here half-filled with Brownies who stared at me as I came in. Some were smiling at me, others were giggling. I smiled back at them which they enjoyed. I got my coffee from a tall blonde that never served me before. She is an attractive friendly woman. Said hello to Shirley. Debbie is also working. I am now finishing up recording the events of Sunday. I showed Paul, on Sunday night, several books that I thought might interest him. I recommended "Dream Power" by Ann Faraday and "Creative Dreaming" by Patricia Garfield. I told Paul that I had been getting much more interested in dreams and their interpretation in the last while. I thought he would also be interested in "The Power Tactics of Jesus Christ" by Haley. I showed him a book "Spiritual Sayings of Kahlil Gibran" which he gave me for Christmas in nineteen-sixty-two, nearly fourteen years ago. He remembered giving me the book. I told him I might as well take the present opportunity to give him back "Human Sex and Sex Education: Perspectives and Problems" by Warren R. Johnson, a book he loaned me many years ago which contains a very sensible rational approach towards sex and sex education. He told me to keep it, that he didn't want it back. He recalled loaning it to me. I highly recommended "A Year of Grace" an anthology of spiritual (in the widest sense) writings by artists, theologians, mystics, etc. of all ages. At about eight p.m. Sunday we went over to Paul's place on Askin Street.

8:15 p.m. Tuesday March 30.
I am at McDonald's on Wellington Road. I just got a second

coffee from a rather pretty little blue-eyed blonde with freckles whose name I can't recall. She is quite friendly. I said hello to Debbie and asked her how she was. She said, "Good and how are you?" I said, "Really great." At Paul's place on Sunday I said hello to and shook hands with Bruna and John who I had not seen in months. The last time I saw Bruna was at the Western Medical School when I introduced her to Barbara. The last time I saw them both together was at the Home County Folk Festival in Victoria Park last August. I also met a friend of theirs who I believe was a medical student studying with John. We ate a Chinese dinner. I was able to eat the fried rice and bean sprouts, bamboo shoots and other vegetables. The meal was really delicious. We had a very good talk while we ate dinner. We got into a discussion of folk music which Bruna and John are really into. They asked me if I was going to see Valdy when he comes to town. I said I couldn't afford to, although I really like Valdy's music. I mentioned that I met Valdy in Montreal at Karma coffee house, the Sir George Williams University coffee house, where I did my first one-man poetry reading.

8:25 p.m. Tuesday March 30.
I'm at McDonald's on Wellington Road. I mentioned to Paul and Niti, Bruna and John, that I got to hear Bob Dylan and The Band in the Montreal Forum. Dylan is John's favourite folk singer. He is also my favourite. I said I had known the members of The Band for around fourteen or fifteen years. They didn't know the group was from around here. I said that Garth Hudson, the musical genius of the group, came from London, went to Medway high school and took music at Western. I said Richard Manuel came from Stratford, Rick Danko from Simcoe, and Robbie Robertson from Toronto. I said the only American was the drummer Levon Helm who came from Arkansas. I said I used to hear them play here in London at the Brass Rail around fifteen years ago when they were called Ronnie Hawkins and the Hawks. I said

Ronnie Hawkins is an old friend of mine from those years. Later on we watched over a hundred slides Paul took of Java and Bali which I enjoyed very much. After the slide show we discussed various techniques and approaches towards self-actualization. I told them about T.M. and Psychosynthesis.

9:50 p.m. Tuesday March 30.
On the Richmond bus heading for downtown. This morning I was photographed by Gordon in the photography studio at Fanshawe. I met Gordon in the cafeteria in the art section where I usually go for coffee when I am at Fanshawe. Later we went to another cafeteria for coffee and after the photographic session we went back there for lunch. We had a very good discussion on photography. I left Fanshawe for home at about two p.m. At home I had some lunch, then went to sleep at about three p.m. because I was really exhausted. I slept till Mary called. Mary and I were just at "Mother's" on Wellington Road. There I introduced Mary and myself to a beautiful dark-haired brown-eyed waitress named Tania. I thought I recognized her from somewhere but she said she has a good memory for faces and would have remembered me. I told her that I might have seen her at Western. She said she goes there to work out so she could have seen me there. I mentioned to Mary when I saw a certain expression on her face that she looked a lot like Linda when Linda made certain facial gestures. I had told Mary before that her facial features reminded me of Linda's facial features in some ways. I told her it was unfortunate that I never got around to introducing her to Linda. She asked me if Linda was still in London. I said that she recently moved to Kincardine. There is so much I want to write and I have only a few minutes left to do it in to keep within my self-imposed time limit.

10:15 p.m. Tuesday March 30.
I am at the Latin Quarter. They have two singers here.

One of them said, "Here's an old Simon and Garfunkel song, 'Last Night I Had the Strangest Dream'." I believe Ed McCurdy, a friend of mine I met at the Jester Coffee House in London, wrote that song. I had a lot of good times at that coffee house which used to be on Richmond Street just north of Oxford. Now they are singing "Suzanne" by Cohen and I flashed on the memory of meeting Leonard at the Winston Churchill pub on Crescent Street in Montreal and later showing him "The Answer Questioned", my pun poem that appeared in "20 Cents Magazine", in the issue with Maureen and I on the cover. So many memories. I said hello to Pauline and Marci and to Jayne who is waiting on my table. It is a really beautiful scene here. Marci asked me how I was. I told her that I felt really great. I said I had done a lot of writing in the past few days that I felt good about. I told Marci about this seven day intensive journal. I explained to her what I was trying to do. She really liked the idea.

10:19 p.m. Tuesday March 30, 1976.
I am at the Latin Quarter drinking a coffee that Jayne brought me. I just asked Jayne if she minded me using her name in my journal book. I told her I write about what happens to me day by day and that I have written about this place and people here including herself. She said she didn't mind at all.

Books Mentioned

Addeo, Edmond G. and Jovita R, *Why Our Children Drink* Prentice-Hall 1975.

Arnold, Les *Rhythms* Applegarth Follies 1975.

Assagioli, Roberto *Psychosynthesis* Viking Compass 1974.

Becker, Ernest *The Denial of Death* The Free Press 1973.

Bell, Don *Saturday Night at the Bagel Factory* McClelland and Stewart 1972.

Bell, Don *Pocketman* Applegarth Follies (forthcoming).

Benedict, Ruth "Forgotten Manuscript" known as *Synergy* and contained in *Peacemaking* by Stanford as described below.

Bloomfield, Cain, Jaffe and Kory *T.M. Discovering Inner Energy and Overcoming Stress* Dell 1975.

Brock, Daniel *Historical Calendar of London* Applegarth Follies 1975.

Buber, Martin *I and Thou* Scribner's 1970.

Conwell, Russell H. *Acres of Diamonds* Harper and Brothers 1943.

Cox, Harvey *The Seduction of the Spirit: The Use and Misue of People's Religion* Simon and Schuster 1973.

Curnoe, Greg ed. *Region* occasional publication by Curnoe in the 1960's.

Dellinger, Dave *More Power Than We Know: The People's Movement Toward Democracy* Doubleday 1975.

Edman, Irwin *The Works of Plato* The Modern Library.

Faraday, Ann *Dream Power* Berkley Medallion Books 1973.

Ferris, Anthony Rizcallah ed. *Spiritual Sayings of Kahlil Gibran* The Citadel Press 1962.

Fuller, Buckminster *I Seem To Be A Verb* Bantam Books 1969.

Fuller, Buckminster *Utopia or Oblivion: The Prospects for Humanity* Bantam Books 1969.

Fuller, Buckminster *An Operating Manual For Spaceship Earth* Dutton 1977.

Garfield, Patricia *Creative Dreaming* Ballantine Books 1976.

Gollancz, Victor ed. *A Year of Grace* Penguin Books 1955.

Goodden, Herman *The Goof* Applegarth Follies 1975.

Grossman, Jack H. *The Business of Living* Stein and Day 1975.

Haley, Jay *The Power Tactics of Jesus Christ* Avon Books 1973.

Harper, Robert *The New Psychotherapies* Prentice-Hall 1975.

Henderson, William *Awakening: Ways to Psycho-Spiritual Growth* Prentice-Hall 1975.

Johnson, Warren R. *Human Sex and Sex Education* Lea and Febiger 1963.

Keen, Sam *To A Dancing God* Harper and Row 1970.

Key, Wilson *Subliminal Seduction* New American Library 1974.

Kiyooka, Roy *Transcanada Letters* Talonbooks 1975.

Kroetsch, Robert *The Ledger* Applegarth Follies 1975.

LeShan, Lawrence *How to Meditate* Bantam Books 1975.

LeShan, Lawrence *The Medium, The Mystic and the Physicist: Toward A General Theory of the Paranormal* Viking Press 1975.

Lowry, Malcolm *Under the Volcano* Penguin Books 1962.

Maltz, Maxwell *Psycho-Cybernetics: A New Way to Get More Living Out of Life* Prentice-Hall 1961.

Maltz, Maxwell and Baker, Raymond Charles *The Conquest of Frustration* Ballantine Books 1976.

McKenzie, Bob ed. *20 Cents Magazine* The Twenty Cents Publishing Company 1969 and 1970.

Miller, Henry *Sexus* Grove 1965.

Munro, Alice *Lives of Girls and Women* McGraw-Hill Ryerson 1974.

Murad, Ahmed *In the Garden: Murshid Sam* Crown Publishers 1975.

Pearce, Joseph Chilton *Exploring the Crack in the Cosmic Egg: Split Minds and Meta-realities* Simon and Schuster 1975.

Pearce, Joseph Chilton *The Crack in the Cosmic Egg: Challenging Constructs of Mind and Reality* Simon and Schuster 1975.

Samuels, Mike and Samuels, Nancy *Seeing With the Mind's Eye: The History Techniques and Uses of Visualization* Random House 1975.

Selye, Hans *The Stress of Life* McGraw-Hill 1956.

Selye, Hans *Stress Without Distress* McClelland and Stewart 1974.

Singer, Jerome *The Inner World of Daydreaming* Harper-Row 1975.

Smith, Adam *Powers of Mind* Random House 1975.

Stanford, Barbara ed. *Peace Making: A Guide to Conflict Resolution for Individuals, Groups, and Nations* Bantam Books 1976.

Thibaudeau, Colleen *Ten Letters* Nairn 1975.

White, John ed. *Frontiers of Consciousness* Avon 1975.

Williams, William Carlos *Kora in Hell* City Lights.

Yevtushenko, Yevgeny *Selected Poems* Penguin Books 1977.

A Note From Roy's Mother

I have known Roy ever since his entry into the world, and it has been interesting, to say the least, following his development through the years.

Roy is outgoing and lovable with a knack for making one feel important and special.

Even so, we do not always see eye to eye, but then who does?

Life has never been dull with Roy around.

But come hell or high water, we will always be the best of friends and be able to converse with each other and enjoy it.

    Good luck Roy.
    Ellen Violet McDonald

About the Author

Born on June 4, 1937, in the evening, at Victoria Hospital, in London, Ontario, Canada. Attended Mountsfield Public School for 8 years. Graduated. Attended South Collegiate Secondary School for 6 years. Didn't graduate. At 17 started taking evening courses at The University of Western Ontario in psychology and later in philosophy. Registered as a non-credit student. Worked at the A&P on Wellington Road, London. At 19 began to write a weekly column called "Thoughts of a Teenager" for The London Free Press. Later the column was called "Impressions". Wrote a weekly series of articles called "Youth in the Pulpit" for the Toronto Sunday Telegram. Also wrote for daily and weekly newspapers across Canada and magazines such as "The Canadian Boy" and "The Calgary Sower". At 25 became initiated into Transcendental Meditation. Lectured on various topics at public schools, high schools, universities, community colleges, church and community groups such as The Unitarian Fellowship and The World Federalists. Was actively involved with the Canadian University Campaign for Nuclear Disarmament, Friends of the Student Non-violent Coordinating Committee, Student Christian Movement, and coalitions against the war in Vietnam. Was involved in Vietnam war protest demonstrations in London, Toronto, Montreal, New York, and Washington. Helped organize and develop discussion programs, plays, poetry readings and other events at coffee houses in Crystal Beach, London, Wasaga Beach and Bala. Was a paid resource person at Rochdale College, a free school in Toronto. At 38 stopped drinking. Free-lance dialogist on college campuses and in coffee houses in London, Toronto, Montreal and other cities. Interested in new developments in humanistic psychology, philosophy, holistic medicine and the development of the total person.